MANCHESTER UNITED

MINUTE
BY MINUTE

Covering More Than 500 Goals,
Penalties, Red Cards and
Other Intriguing Facts

DAVID JACKSON

First published by Pitch Publishing, 2021

Pitch Publishing
A2 Yeoman Gate
Yeoman Way
Worthing
Sussex
BN13 3QZ
www.pitchpublishing.co.uk
info@pitchpublishing.co.uk

ISBN 978 1 78531 843 6

Typesetting and origination by Pitch Publishing
Printed and bound in India by Replika Press Pvt. Ltd

Contents

For Jeff Withington,
And for Fiona and Darren

Acknowledgements

Manchester United: Minute by Minute was a hard but hugely enjoyable book to research, and thanks to certain resource outlets it was made a lot easier.

The goal times are taken from various resources. BBC Scotland match reports, Sky Sports games, endless YouTube highlights (and countless newspaper clippings and old match reports that sometimes tested my eyesight to the limit), plus United's official website and various other fan sites and stats platforms such as Opta, Soccerbase, Transfermarkt and 11v11 all proved helpful.

Finally, I'd like to thank Paul and Jane Camillin – the tireless siblings who mastermind Pitch Publishing – for green-lighting this series. Having a *Manchester United: Minute by Minute* was a no-brainer and, we have an end result.

Introduction

Manchester United have an extraordinary history and *Manchester United: Minute by Minute* takes you through the Reds' matchday history and records the historic goals, incidents, memorable moments, and the minute they happened in.

From United's early beginnings and successes to the days of domestic domination; from the Busby Babes era, the colourful spells under Tommy Docherty and Ron Atkinson to the incredible Sir Alex Ferguson years.

Learn about the club's most historic moments or simply relive some truly unforgettable matches from the Reds' history, from the first game as Newton Heath to the present day and everything in between.

Included are all the First Division and Premier League successes, the FA Cup, League Cup, FA Charity Shield triumphs and, of course, United's numerous European – and world – crowns over the years.

Games played on the world's biggest stages – the Camp Nou, San Siro, Wembley Stadium, the Millennium Stadium, Anfield, the Bernabéu, Maine Road, the Etihad Stadium, Highbury, plus a few played at Old Trafford too.

You will also discover just how many times a crucial goal has been scored at the same minute over the years

– and why so few are scored in the 36th minute. From goals scored in the opening few seconds to the last-gasp extra-time winners, and the drama of numerous penalty shoot-outs that have thrilled generations of fans at Old Trafford or around the world, all are featured.

Included are countless goals from Denis Law, George Best, Bobby Charlton, Stuart Pearson, Frank Stapleton, Ruud van Nistelrooy, Wayne Rooney, David Beckham, Cristiano Ronaldo, Dimitar Berbatov and Ryan Giggs up to Bruno Fernandes and Marcus Rashford as well as a cast of hundreds who have played for United and including many players who may not have hit the heights, but have still played their part in in the Reds' history – names such as Kieran Lee and Federico Macheda, who are included in the pages that follow but might have drifted out of the memory with the passage of time.

Now you can discover just when those historic, brilliant, dramatic, or occasionally even seemingly run-of-the-mill goals were scored and how they were created. Moments – not all good – when games swing this way or that, with pivotal goals, penalties or even red cards – everything that matters historically and that have helped shape the destiny of Manchester United Football Club.

And finally, we reveal the truth behind the so-called 'Fergie Time' element to so many of United's crucial goals – is it fact or a myth?

Enjoy, relive and recall.

Minute by Minute

And we're off ...

19 seconds

1 December 2004

David Bellion puts United ahead within seconds of the kick-off to open up a 1-0 lead that will be enough to see off Arsenal in the League Cup quarter-final at Old Trafford. With both United and Arsenal playing largely second-string sides, the Reds strike when a Johan Djourou mistake allows Bellion to aim a weak shot towards goal and it somehow squeezes through keeper Manuel Almunia and into the net.

31 seconds

22 December 2001

Ruud van Nistelrooy scores in United's first attack with the Southampton defenders caught well and truly cold. There seems little threat when Paul Scholes receives the ball on the left flank at the halfway line – but Scholes plays an angled, pinpoint 40-yard pass to van Nistelrooy on the edge of the Saints box and after controlling the ball, the Dutchman lashes a low right-footed shot across the keeper and into the bottom-left corner as the Reds go 1-0 up.

32 seconds

28 November 2012

Robin van Persie puts United 1-0 up against West Ham in the first attack of the game. Michael Carrick finds the Dutchman on the edge of the Hammers' box and he uses the pace of the pass to flick the ball over Winston Reid and then hits a shot that takes a wicked deflection off James Collins, looping over the grounded Jussi Jaaskelainen and into the net for a bizarre but welcome start at Old Trafford.

34 seconds

7 March 2021

United are awarded the fastest Manchester derby penalty of all time with barely half a minute played of the clash with Manchester City at the Etihad. Anthony Martial moves past a couple of challenges on the edge of the box before Gabriel Jesus clips his heels and the referee points to the spot in what is an unbelievable start for the Reds.

36 seconds

9 May 2011

In a game neither can afford to lose, United go 1-0 up against Chelsea inside the first minute in what is effectively a title-decider at Old Trafford. The Reds went in three points clear of the visitors with just three matches to play but couldn't have dreamed of a better start. With only 36 second on the clock, Ji-Sung Park threads a pass into the path of Javier Hernandez and the Mexican races clear before tucking a low ball to the left of Petr Cech to make it 1-0 and send Old Trafford wild.

52 seconds

11 December 2011

Wayne Rooney ends a wonderful United passing move by putting the Reds 1-0 up inside the first minute away to Queens Park Rangers. Rooney nods the ball wide to the right for Antonio Valencia, who then finds the forward's run into the box with a fine cross that is headed purposely to the left of the keeper who has no chance.

1

14 January 2009

Wayne Rooney scores what will prove to be the winning goal in the first minute of the Reds' home game with Wigan Athletic. Rooney slides home Cristiano Ronaldo's tempting low cross and, with no further goals for either side in the 89 minutes plus stoppage time that remained, he gives United a 1-0 victory and reduces the gap to Premier League leaders Liverpool to just two points.

2

6 May 1967

Needing a point to clinch the First Division title, United get off to an unbelievable start away to West Ham United. With Sir Matt Busby still to take his place on the bench, the Reds pour forward and Bobby Charlton fires home to make it 1-0 at Upton Park on a day that will be unforgettable for all United fans. Sir Matt took his place moments later, not even realising his side had taken the lead and assumed the Hammers were kicking the game off!

28 November 1990

United take just 80 seconds to break the deadlock against Arsenal in the League Cup third round at Highbury. A free kick is awarded 25 yards from goal and Paul Ince taps the ball to Clayton Blackmore, who drills a right-footed shot low and hard into the bottom-left corner of David Seaman's net to put the Reds 1-0 up.

6 February 1999

On what will be an unforgettable day at the City Ground, United go ahead inside two minutes against Nottingham Forest. The hosts, rooted to the foot of the table and under new management in the shape of ex-United boss Ron Atkinson, are opened up when a corner is cleared out to the right where Roy Keane collects – he plays a short pass back to Paul Scholes on the edge of the box and his first-time cross is met with a low volley from Dwight Yorke from six yards to make it 1-0.

18 November 2000

The first Premier League Manchester derby for more than four years sees United take the lead after just 95 seconds. In what is the 125th meeting of the Blues and the Reds, the game starts at breakneck speed and when Alfie Inge Haaland clatters into Paul Scholes, United have a chance to break the deadlock. With David Beckham on the pitch, anything is possible so when the newly appointed England captain curls a 30-yard free kick past Nicky Weaver, even the City fans aren't that surprised. It will be the only goal of an entertaining game.

20 September 2009

United score one of the earliest Manchester derby goals on record to go 1-0 up against City at Old Trafford. In an explosive start, Patrice Evra weaves his way to the left of the City six-yard box where Wayne Rooney feigns to shoot before cleverly nudging the ball past two defenders and drilling home a low shot under keeper Shay Given from five yards.

30 March 2010

United get off to the perfect start in the Champions League quarter-final first leg away to Bayern Munich. The Germans are caught cold when Nani's corner comes in and after two Bayern players collide, it leaves Wayne Rooney with acres of space to head the ball home from a couple of yards out.

27 November 2010

Dimitar Berbatov starts what will be a very good day when he prods home from a couple of yards out against Blackburn Rovers. The Bulgarian is razor-sharp as Nani's cross from the left is flicked on by Wayne Rooney and Berbatov gets in front of his marker to volley home and put United 1-0 up.

9 January 2011

Ryan Giggs puts United ahead in the FA Cup third round at home to Liverpool. With only 30 seconds on the clock, Daniel Agger's challenge on Dimitar Berbatov is deemed a foul by the referee and Giggs steps up to make it 1-0 in a tie that will later see Steven Gerrard sent off. The penalty turns out to be the only goal of a game that marks Kenny Dalglish's return as Anfield boss.

22 April 2013

On a day when the Reds know victory will guarantee a record 20th top flight title, Robin van Persie scores in just the second minute. The move that leads to the goal starts when Wayne Rooney sprays a superb 40-yard pass out to Antonio Valencia on the right flank – he plays it back to Rafael and sends a deep cross towards the back post where Ryan Giggs volleys it back across the face of goal and van Persie has the easiest of tap-ins from two yards out to put United 1-0 up against Aston Villa.

6 March 2019

Trailing 2-0 to Paris St Germain from the Champions League round of 16 first leg at Old Trafford, United get off to a dream start in the second leg in Paris. Romelu Lukaku manages to intercept a poor back-pass but still has plenty to do as he takes on the keeper, rounds him and then has to slide an acute angled shot into the net to halve the deficit and set the tone for what would be a famous European night for Ole Gunnar Solskjaer's young side.

20 December 2020

In what will be a goal fest at Old Trafford, United take a 1-0 lead against Leeds United.

The Reds attack down the left and Bruno Fernandes cuts in towards the box before spotting the burst forward by Scott McTominay, to whom he lays a square pass, and the young Scot fizzes a low daisy-cutter into the bottom-right corner from the edge of the box.

7 March 2021

Bruno Fernandes puts United 1-0 up in the Manchester derby at the Etihad. City's Gabriel Jesus had fouled Anthony Martial just inside the box and referee Anthony Taylor awarded a spot-kick. After a VAR check, Fernandes tucks the ball to Ederson's right and though the Brazilian gets a hand to the shot, it still has enough power to go into the net.

3

6 September 1972

Though nobody knew at the time, Denis Law's early goal away to Oxford United will be his last for Manchester United. The one-time record signing, in his 11th campaign with the Reds, scores goal No.237 at the Manor Ground to put United 1-0 up – though Oxford will level a minute later!

25 February 2001

Dwight Yorke opens the scoring in an unforgettable United performance at home to title rivals Arsenal. What will become a one-sided rout begins when Denis Irwin plays a pass to the feet of Yorke on the edge of the area and his ball to Paul Scholes sees the midfielder pushed wide to the right of the six-yard box, but his only intention is to cross to Yorke at the far post – which he does – and Yorke bundles home his first of the afternoon.

12 September 2008

United take the lead at Anfield to silence to Kop with a fine Carlos Tevez goal. The Reds attack down the right and when Dimitar Berbatov gets into the box, his precision low ball back towards the edge of the Liverpool box is powerfully side-footed home by Tevez from 15 yards to put United 1-0 up.

1 November 2008

Brilliant improvisation by Cristiano Ronaldo results in United taking an early lead against Hull City at Old Trafford. The visitors, unbeaten away from home in the Premier League and two points ahead of the Reds going into the game, are caught cold when Ronaldo cushions a long ball into the Tigers' box with an impudent flick back out to Dimitar Berbatov – the Bulgarian then fizzes a low ball back to Ronaldo on the edge of the box and he takes one touch before firing a low shot just inside the right post to make it 1-0 for the hosts.

7 April 2010

The Reds take just three minutes to erase Bayern Munich's Champions League quarter-final first leg lead. Wayne Rooney drives towards goal before playing a short pass to his right where Darron Gibson collects and then, as he spots the keeper slightly out of position, Gibson hits a low shot from 20 yards that goes into the bottom-right corner to make it 1-0 on the night and 2-2 on aggregate at Old Trafford.

3 November 2012

Robin van Persie takes just three minutes to remind Arsenal fans what they are missing as he puts the Reds 1-0 up at Old Trafford. The Dutch striker's high-profile move from the Gunners continues to be a huge success as Rafael's cross is poorly cleared by Thomas Vermaelen into his former team-mate's path where he hits a low, angled shot inside the left post from 15 yards.

11 August 2018

United start the 2018/19 Premier League campaign with a goal after just three minutes against Leicester City. The Reds are awarded a penalty when Daniel Amartey handles Alexis Sanchez's deflected shot and the referee points to the spot. Captain for the day Paul Pogba steps up to fire a shot into the top-left corner, giving keeper Kasper Schmeichel no chance and putting José Mourinho's men 1-0 up at Old Trafford.

25 September 2018

United take the lead against Derby County with a sweeping move that leaves the Championship side reeling. Anthony Martial's burst down the left flank sees the French forward play in a low cross that is flicked by Romelu Lukaku and nudged on into the path of Juan Mata by Jesse Lingard. The Spaniard makes no mistake with a low shot into the bottom-left corner from 12 yards to make it 1-0 in the League Cup third round tie.

20 December 2020

Anthony Martial is the provider as United's superb start against Leeds continues at Old Trafford. The French forward slips a clever through ball into the box and Scott McTominay runs on and hits a low shot across the keeper into the bottom corner to grab his second and put the Reds 2-0 up in double-quick time.

4

30 August 1999

Andy Cole comes back to haunt his former club Newcastle United as he hits the first of four goals – fittingly in the fourth minute – against the Magpies. Dwight Yorke plays a pass to Cole on the edge of the box and an untidy one-two ensues as he manages to play it to Paul Scholes whose return ball leaves Cole with just Tommy Wright to beat, which he does easily to make it 1-0 at Old Trafford.

11 September 1999

United get off to the perfect start at Anfield. Dwight Yorke lays the ball left to Ryan Giggs and his cross from the left of the Liverpool box is superbly headed into the bottom-right corner – by Jamie Carragher. The Liverpool defender's finish gives his keeper no chance in front of a stunned Kop as the Reds go 1-0 up.

11 March 2009

A soaring goal from Nemanja Vidic gets United up and running in the Champions League round of 16 second leg against Inter Milan at Old Trafford. Having drawn the first leg 0-0 in Italy, the Reds are looking for the early goal that will set the tone for the game and when Ryan Giggs's corner comes in from the right, Vidic connects perfectly to head into the left corner from eight yards out – a superb goal.

5

24 April 2007

United get off to a dream start in the Champions League semi-final first leg against AC Milan with a set-piece goal. A corner whipped in from the right sees Cristiano Ronaldo leap to head goalwards. The keeper manages to get a hand on it but only pushes the ball up and Gabriel Heinze leaps to try and ensure it crosses the line – but it does anyway without him getting any contact – to put the Reds ahead at Old Trafford.

10 March 2003

The brilliance of Michael Carrick results in the opening goal of the FA Cup quarter-final against Chelsea. Tom Cleverley finds Carrick with a short pass just inside the Chelsea half and the United midfielder takes a quick glance ahead and then lofts a perfect ball into the run of Javier Hernandez, who loops his header up and over Petr Cech – who hadn't known whether to stick or twist – and into the right of the net to make it 1-0 at Old Trafford.

6

9 March 1966

United get off to the perfect start in the European quarter-final, second-leg tie against Benfica. After narrowly beating the Portuguese 3-2 at Old Trafford. The Reds soon take the lead when Tony Dunne's free kick on the left flank is sent into the Benfica box and George Best leaps to head over the onrushing keeper and into the top right-hand corner to give United a priceless away goal and make it 1-0 on the night.

3 March 1999

Dwight Yorke gives United a great start in the Champions League quarter-final first leg against Inter Milan. As so often happens, David Beckham provides the ideal ball into the box and Yorke sends a diving angled header past the keeper and into the bottom-right corner to send Old Trafford wild.

9 December 2006

Wayne Rooney scores to put United 1-0 up against Manchester City at Old Trafford. The Reds are at City from the kick-off and when Cristiano Ronaldo's excellent low, arcing cross from the right finds Rooney's burst into the box, he sweeps the ball past keeper Nicky Weaver and into the bottom-right corner.

16 April 2009

A stunning effort from Cristiano Ronaldo will be enough to send United into the Champions League semi-finals as he scores the only goal of the second leg against Porto, with the aggregate score 2-2 from the first leg. When Anderson plays a short ball to Ronaldo just inside the Porto half, there seems little threat for the home side but after teeing himself up, Ronaldo unleashes a 35-yard shot that flies into the top-left corner to make it 1-0 – the score that wins the game for United.

19 May 2013

On what will be an extraordinary afternoon at The Hawthorns, United take an early lead against West Bromwich Albion. The Reds, bidding farewell to Sir Alex Ferguson on his 1,500th game in charge, get off to a flyer when Javier Hernandez, out near the right-hand corner flag, spots Shinji Kagawa in the box, crosses in and the Japanese international heads home to make it 1-0.

11 August 2013

Robin van Persie puts David Moyes's United 1-0 up against Wigan Athletic in the FA Community Shield at Wembley. And it's a goal worthy of opening any season as the Premier League champions take on the FA Cup winners. Patrice Evra sends a cross in from the left flank and van Persie rises to send a superb header into the bottom-left corner from ten yards, giving keeper Scott Carson no chance.

7

18 August 1962

British transfer record signing Denis Law takes just seven minutes to score his first goal for United. The Scottish striker, signed for £115,000 from Torino, is the star attraction for the 51,685 Old Trafford crowd and his typically predatory goal puts the Reds 2-0 up against West Brom, with David Herd having scored inside the first minute.

23 April 1977

Former Stoke City striker Jimmy Greenhoff opens the scoring in the FA Cup semi-final against Leeds United at Hillsborough. United win a corner on the right after Steve Coppell's cross is blocked and Gordon Hill's flag-kick is nodded backwards by Stewart Houston and as a Leeds defender mis-kicks his clearance, Greenhoff pounces, shooting the loose ball high into the roof of the net to make it 1-0 to the Reds in the War of the Roses.

4 November 1998

Brondby must fear the worst as they concede after just seven minutes of the return Champions League group stage clash against United. The Danes had been beaten 6-2 on their own soil a fortnight before. David Beckham starts what will be part two of the rout with a superb free kick from 30 yards – the England midfielder whips a curling shot into the bottom-left corner from 25 yards to put his side 1-0 up at Old Trafford.

6 February 1999

In a fast and furious start at the City Ground, United immediately respond to Nottingham Forest's equaliser by retaking the lead. Chasing a long pass out of defence, Andy Cole runs between two defenders and gets to the ball first, knocking it past the keeper before slotting the ball home from the right of the six-yard box to put the Reds 2-1 up in a breathless start in the East Midlands.

7 April 2010

A brilliant piece of improvisation puts United 2-0 up inside seven minutes after a scintillating start to the Champions League quarter-final second leg. Bayern Munich had led 2-1 from the first leg but the Reds are ahead on aggregate in double-quick time as the scorer of the first goal – Darron Gibson – fizzes in a low cross from the right and Nani flicks the ball with the inside of his right heel to send the ball into the bottom-right corner of the net.

8

26 September 1956

Tommy Taylor opens the scoring for United on what will be a record-breaking win. Facing Anderlecht in the second leg of a European Cup preliminary round, Taylor opens the floodgates as he makes it 1-0 against the Belgians – but because Old Trafford's floodlights weren't ready, this will turn into a record 10-0 win at Maine Road, home of Manchester City, where the midweek tie had to be played!

7 August 1993

Mark Hughes puts United 1-0 up in the FA Charity Shield clash with Arsenal. The opening goal at a hot and sunny Wembley Stadium comes when Denis Irwin's cross towards the far post is knocked back into the middle where Hughes spectacularly volleys into the bottom-left corner to put the Reds in command.

22 April 2000

Needing three points to seal a sixth Premier League title in eight years, United are awarded a free kick on the edge of the box. David Beckham steps up to hit an unstoppable curling shot around the wall and into the top-right corner to put the Reds ahead at Southampton and on course for glory.

20 August 2006

United start the 2006/07 season as they mean to go on with a blistering display against Fulham at Old Trafford. In front of an opening-day crowd in excess of 75,000, the Reds are quick out of the blocks and a superb Ryan Giggs cross from the left sees Louis Saha ghost between Ian Pearce and Liam Rosenior to head down powerfully past the keeper from five yards.

5 May 2009

United get a priceless early goal in the second leg of the Champions League semi-final at the Emirates to go 2-0 ahead on aggregate. Arsenal concede when Cristiano Ronaldo's cut-back in the box from the left sees Kieran Gibbs slip at the worst possible moment and Ji-Sung Park is able to easily round the grounded defender and then fire a shot into the roof of the net from close range to put the Reds firmly in the driving seat.

22 March 2014

A stunning Wayne Rooney goal puts United 1-0 up away to West Ham at Upton Park. This is one for the scrapbook as a pass bounces towards him on the halfway line and he eases James Tomkins out of the way before half-volleying a 50-yard lob (with plenty of slice on it) over a disorientated Adrian in the Hammers goal and into the net for an incredible piece of individual skill. The goal draws comparisons with one David Beckham scored against Crystal Palace.

9

6 May 1967

United go 2-0 up away to West Ham in a game that will see the Reds crowned champions of England for the second time in three years. Needing a point to win the title for a seventh time and leading through Bobby Charlton's second-minute goal, Paddy Crerand scores a rare header to double the Reds' lead against the Hammers – his third goal of the campaign.

18 December 1999

David Beckham uses the jeers and abuse from the West Ham fans to inspire him as he sets United on the way to victory at Upton Park. Beckham, on the right flank, curls in a perfect cross into the box that Dwight Yorke expertly nods past Shaka Hislop to put the Reds 1-0 up.

30 March 2002

The Reds get their noses in front in the War of the Roses clash at Elland Road. In a game that rarely disappoints, United work an opening when a crossfield ball finds Mikael Silvestre on the left of the Leeds box. He checks inside one challenge and spots Paul Scholes free on the penalty spot, plays a pass just in front and Scholes fires a low shot into the right of the goal and past the keeper to make it 1-0.

19 May 2013

Jonas Olsson's desperate attempt to clear Antonio Valencia's rasping low cross results in the West Brom defenders diverting the ball past his own keeper as United take a 2-0 lead at The Hawthorns.

16 August 2020

Bruno Fernandes tucks home United's 22nd penalty of the elongated 2019/20 campaign to give the Reds a 1-0 Europa League semi-final lead over Sevilla in Cologne. In what is United's third semi-final of the season having reached the same stage of the FA Cup and League Cup, Ole Gunnar Solskjaer's side are awarded a spot-kick when Diego Carlos fouls Marcus Rashford in the box and Fernandes makes no mistake from 12 yards.

10

8 January 2012

Still smarting from the 6-1 home defeat to Manchester City ten weeks earlier, the FA Cup third round tie at the Etihad offered United the chance of erasing some of that pain and it is clear from the kick-off how much pent-up frustration there had been within the Reds camp. The first goal would be crucial in this battle of the Manchester giants and it goes United's way when Wayne Rooney collects the ball midway inside the City half and then plays it out to Antonio Valencia on the right flank. Valencia's first-time cross is met on the full by the head of Rooney who had continued his run into the box and his effort arrows past City keeper Costel Pantilimon and in off the underside of the bar to make it 1-0 at the Etihad.

9 August 2009

A spectacular long-range effort from Nani puts United 1-0 up against Chelsea in the FA Community Shield at Wembley. The annual season curtain-raiser, played in glorious north London sunshine, explodes into life when the Portuguese winger cuts in from the left before striking a stunning angled shot from 25 yards that flies past Petr Cech into the bottom-right corner of the net.

20 April 2017

Henrikh Mkhitaryan puts United ahead in the Europa League quarter-final second leg against Anderlecht. After a draw in the first leg in Belgium, the return clash at Old Trafford proves just as tight but when Marcus Rashford's attempt to cross from the left is blocked back to him he instead plays a short pass to Mkhitaryan, who sets himself up and then fires a low shot into the bottom-left corner to put the Reds 1-0 up.

11

22 May 1999

Barely two minutes after coming on as a replacement for the injured Roy Keane, Teddy Sheringham opens the scoring for treble-chasing United in the 1999 FA Cup Final against Newcastle United. Andy Cole finds Sheringham who is surrounded by Newcastle defenders, but he nutmegs one and then toe-pokes a pass to Paul Scholes before running into space for the return. Scholes duly plays the perfect ball into Sheringham's path and the former Spurs striker hits a low shot through keeper Steve Harper's legs and into the bottom-left corner to put the Reds 1-0 up at Wembley. It is also Sheringham's 250th career goal – what a way to reach the landmark.

3 May 2003

United edge ever closer to the Premier League title as David Beckham opens the scoring against Charlton Athletic. Knowing victory will put the Reds within two points of being crowned champions, Beckham hits a deflected rising shot past the keeper and into the left of the net to make it 1-0.

10 April 2007

Michael Carrick's first European goal gives United a 1-0 lead against Roma in the Champions League. The

Reds trail 2-1 from the first leg, but Carrick levels the aggregate score when Cristiano Ronaldo's trickery on the right sees the Portuguese winger play the ball inside to Carrick, who spots the keeper off his line and hits a 25-yard chip into the top-right corner.

5 May 2009

United silence the Emirates as Cristiano Ronaldo scores a superb angled free kick from fully 35 yards out. The Portuguese winger – who had scored from a similar distance against Porto in the quarter-finals – hits a shot from the right, midway inside the Gunners' half, and the ball swerves and dips though is never more than hip height. It fools Manuel Almunia who goes too low in his attempt to save it as it fizzes over his head. It puts the Reds 2-0 up on the night and 3-0 up on aggregate with only 11 minutes of the Champions League semi-final second leg played. It means the Gunners need to find four goals in the time that remains.

19 November 2011

United make it three successive 1-0 victories in a row since the 6-1 home defeat to Manchester City. The Reds had needed to dig deep to get back on track after that sobering loss to the Blues but three clean sheets told their own story and away to Swansea City, Javier Hernandez is again the fox in the box as he taps home from close range from Ryan Giggs's cross following a mistake by Angel Rangel.

10 March 2003

United look to be on the way to the FA Cup semi-final when Wayne Rooney doubles their lead with just 11 minutes on the clock. It's a clever set piece that makes it 2-0, with Rooney whipping a curling free kick on the left, just outside the Chelsea box – such is the pace and swerve that Petr Cech decides to stay on his line but when the ball clears the heads of everyone, it bounces once and goes into the far right corner. Despite the flying start, Chelsea will score twice after the break to force a replay at Stamford Bridge.

12

28 February 2010

Despite falling behind to a fifth-minute James Milner penalty, United level on 12 minutes in the 2010 League Cup Final against Aston Villa. Dimitar Berbatov dispossesses former Manchester City skipper Richard Dunne midway inside the Villa half and runs towards the box. Dunne recovers to nick the ball away from Berbatov but it rolls into the path of Michael Owen, who fires a low shot into the bottom-left corner from 12 yards out to make it 1-1.

8 January 2012

Having just taken the lead in the FA Cup third round away to City, United are given a huge fillip as Blues' influential skipper Vincent Kompany is shown a straight red card for a challenge that saw the Belgian slide in with both feet to dispossess Nani. Referee Chris Foy deems it a 'studs-up' tackle and sends Kompany off, though it fairness Nani hardly complained, wasn't injured and the incessant Manchester rain all had to be considered. No matter – City were down to ten men and had lost their skipper.

13

6 March 1966

A superb individual goal by George Best puts United 2-0 up away to Benfica at the Stadium of Light. A long ball into the Portuguese half sees John Connelly cleverly head back to Best, who collects the ball and takes it past two players with his first touch, bursting into the Benfica box before drilling a low, right-footed shot across the keeper and into the bottom left corner to put the Reds 5-2 up on aggregate.

4 November 1998

Andy Cole doubles United's lead against Brondby. Strike partner Dwight Yorke lays a ball off to Cole who deftly chips a shot over the diving keeper from the left of the six-yard box to make it 2-0 at Old Trafford. A delightful finish.

18 December 1999

United's blistering start at Upton Park continues with a second goal. The West Ham defenders are like rabbits caught in the headlights as Dwight Yorke crosses for Ryan Giggs to toe-poke the ball past Shaka Hislop and put the Reds 2-0 up in quickfire fashion against the Hammers.

5 April 2009

Cristiano Ronaldo fires United ahead against Aston Villa with a clever free kick. After an infringement inside the box and to the left of goal, Ryan Giggs rolls the ball to Ronaldo who curls a shot into the top-right corner to give the title-chasing Reds an early advantage.

14

12 April 1992

United win the League Cup for the first time since the competition began some 32 years before. Taking on Brian Clough's Nottingham Forest at Wembley, the only goal of the game comes when Gary Pallister plays the ball midway inside the Forest half to Brian McClair, who in turn lays it off to Ryan Giggs. Giggs moves with purpose towards the Forest defence, creating space for McClair as a result, and then the Welsh winger plays a side pass to McClair who dribbles into the Forest box before firing a shot past keeper Andy Marriott into the bottom-right corner of the net. Forest, four-times winners of the competition, cannot find a way back into the final, which ends 1-0.

29 April 2008

United, having held Barcelona 0-0 at the Camp Nou in the first leg of the Champions League semi-final, look to get the early advantage that could swing the tie. In the battle of two of European football's entertainers, this was the game many neutrals had wanted for the final, but as it was, the winners would face either Liverpool or Chelsea in Moscow. The Reds had survived an early penalty claim when Paul Scholes tripped Lionel Messi and take the lead in spectacular fashion. Gianluca Zambrotta's misplaced clearance is quickly intercepted by Scholes, who takes one touch before hitting a swerving 25-yard thunderbolt that gives Barca keeper Victor Valdes no chance as it sails into the top-right corner to put the Reds 1-0 up and send Old Trafford wild. It will prove to be the only goal of a nail-biting game and send United into a first all-English Champions League Final, against Chelsea.

12 April 2015

Ashley Young levels for United against Manchester City in a rip-roaring start to the Old Trafford Manchester derby. City had gone ahead on six minutes but Young equalises when Ander Herrera's low cross sees Gael Clichy's attempted clearance fall kindly for the wingers who reacts first to poke home from a couple of yards out.

10 March 2018

Marcus Rashford puts United 1-0 up at home to Liverpool with a typically inventive and clinical finish. Chasing a Romelu Lukaku flick-on from David de Gea's goal kick, Rashford gets into the Liverpool box and cleverly cuts inside Trent Alexander-Arnold before curling a powerful, angled shot across the keeper and inside the right post to the delight of the Old Trafford crowd.

15

23 April 1977

United's dream start to the FA Cup semi-final with Leeds United at Hillsborough continues as Steve Coppell makes it 2-0. The Reds attack down the left and when a loose ball comes to left-winger Gordon Hill, his shot is blocked but falls kindly for right-winger Coppell who half-volleys a shot into the top-left corner to put United in a commanding position – one that Jimmy Armfield's Leeds will never fully recover from, despite a second-half goal from Allan Clarke.

4 March 1995

Mark Hughes is the architect as United begin a memorable afternoon at home to Ipswich Town in the Premier League. Hughes collects the ball on the left of the Ipswich box and weighs up his options before playing a cross to Roy Keane on the edge of the box. The Reds' skipper fires a low shot in off the left-hand post and into the back of the net on what will be a long afternoon for the Tractor Boys.

22 April 2000

United double their lead at The Dell against Southampton. Knowing victory will guarantee yet another Premier League title, the Reds are already 1-0 up when Phil Neville attacks down the left before hitting a low cross towards the six-yard box where Francis Benali – caught in two minds – sticks out a boot and deflects it past his own keeper to make it 2-0 to the champions-elect.

10 August 2003

United take the lead against Arsenal in the 2003 FA Charity Shield at Cardiff's Millennium Stadium – the Reds' 22nd appearance in the annual curtain-raiser. It's a set-piece that undoes the Gunners, as Ryan Giggs's right-wing corner is flicked on by Roy Keane and Mikael Silvestre heads home from close range to make it 1-0.

7 April 2009

Having been stunned by a Porto goal on four minutes, United get back on level terms to make it 1-1 in the Champions League quarter-final first leg at Old Trafford. The Reds had conceded after a series of blunders first from Cristiano Ronaldo and then Jonny Evans – but the Portuguese side gift the hosts an equaliser when Porto defender Bruno Alves doesn't look as he passes the ball back to his keeper and Wayne Rooney easily intercepts before tucking a low shot home.

16

4 November 1998

Phil Neville puts United 3-0 up against Brondby after a sweet 16 opening minutes of the Champions League group stage clash at Old Trafford. Neville collects the ball on the edge of the Danes' box before drilling a low right-foot shot into the bottom-right corner for only his second United goal.

20 August 2006

A third goal in eight minutes as a rampant United tear Fulham's defence to shreds yet again. Just as with the first two, Louis Saha is involved and yet again, the goal comes from a cross into the box. Gary Neville's excellent cross from the right is volleyed goalwards by Saha from point blank range and despite a fine reflex save from the keeper, Wayne Rooney is on hand to put the loose ball into the back of the net to make it 3-0.

9 December 2012

United snatch an early lead in the Manchester derby at the Etihad. Ashley Young breaks into the City half before feeding Wayne Rooney with a short pass on the edge of the box. Rooney appears to scuff a low shot that goes through the legs of Gareth Barry, wrong-foots Joe Hart and trickles into the bottom-left corner of the net to put the Premier League leaders 1-0 up against the defending champions.

17

16 September 1998

United take the lead against Barcelona on a raucous night at Old Trafford. In what is the opening Champions League group stage clash, the Reds – who should have already been ahead but for an astonishing miss by Ole Gunnar Solskjaer – do score when David Beckham's cross from the right is headed home by Ryan Giggs.

14 April 1999

A stunning David Beckham strike puts United 1-0 up in the FA Cup semi-final replay against Arsenal at Villa Park. The Gunners had been the better side in the opening exchanges but it is the Reds who draw first blood with a counter-attack that sees Teddy Sheringham find Beckham 25 yards from goal and his swerving first-time shot flies past the keeper.

10 April 2007

Old Trafford celebrates as United go 2-0 up against Roma. Having already cancelled out the Italians' first-leg lead, the Reds edge ahead when Ryan Giggs plays a pass towards Alan Smith, and when a Roma defender mis-hits his clearance it falls to Smith who hits a crisp shot past the keeper and into the right of the net to make it 2-0 in the Champions League quarter-final second leg.

It is Smith's first goal at Old Trafford for almost two and a half years.

29 April 2009

United's incessant pressure from kick-off is rewarded with a goal as John O'Shea gives the Reds the lead in the all-England Champions League semi-final first leg at Old Trafford against Arsenal. The Gunners were fortunate not to already be behind thanks to some brilliant goalkeeping from Manuel Almunia, but the breakthrough had to come sooner or later and when Arsenal fail to clear a corner, Michael Carrick gets to the ball on the left of the box and his low cross finds its way through to O'Shea who rifles a thumping drive into the roof of the net from seven yards out. It will be the only goal of the game as United look to defend their Champions League crown.

19 January 2010

Ryan Giggs scores his first Manchester derby goal for 14 years as he gives the Reds an early advantage in the League Cup semi-final first leg at the Etihad. Antonio Valencia squeezes past Craig Bellamy's challenge on the left of the box before crossing low into the six-yard area for Wayne Rooney to flick towards goal – the shot rolls across the face of the goal where Giggs has the easiest of tap-ins to make it 1-0.

11 May 2017

Marouane Fellaini scores the goal that will prove good enough to secure United a spot in the 2017 Europa

League Final. After winning the first leg of the semi-final 1-0 in Spain, the Reds double their advantage when Marcus Rashford, midway inside the Celta Vigo half, checks inside before sending a cross into the box for Fellaini to expertly guide past the keeper and make it 1-0 on the night and 2-0 on aggregate. Though Celta will later level and both sides end with ten men, the Reds edge home 2-1 overall.

18

11 September 1999

United go 2-0 up against Liverpool. David Beckham sends a free kick in from the right flank and Andy Cole gets up highest to head down and past the keeper to put the Reds firmly in control of the Premier League clash at a hushed Anfield.

25 February 2001

United regain the lead against Arsenal in a top-of-the-table clash at Old Trafford. Dwight Yorke had opened the scoring and Thierry Henry levelled shortly after – but Yorke strikes again as Roy Keane's pass from the halfway line sees him race clear and fire a low left-footed shot past the keeper to make it 2-1.

24 May 2017

United take the lead in the 2017 Europa League Final in Sweden. Up against Dutch giants Ajax, it's the first time the Reds have reached the final in the competition formerly known as the UEFA Cup and it is José Mourinho's side who strike first when Marouane Fellaini plays a short ball to Paul Pogba on the edge of the box.

Pogba shifts to his left before firing a fierce drive that strikes Davinson Sánchez, loops up and wrong-foots keeper André Onana on its way into the centre of the net.

2 February 2021

The start of what will be a long evening for Southampton who had been reduced to ten men after just two minutes as United open the scoring in the Premier League fixture at Old Trafford. Marcus Rashford evades a challenge on the left of the Saints penalty area and lays the ball back to Luke Shaw, whose first-time cross into the six-yard box finds Aaron Wan-Bissaka arriving on cue to send a low, right-footed volley through the keeper's legs and make it 1-0.

19

4 March 1995

Brilliant wing play by Ryan Giggs results in United going 2-0 up against Ipswich Town as the Reds score a second goal in four minutes. Giggs intercepts play down the left flank before racing towards the visitors' box and sending a measured low cross into the middle where Andy Cole expertly slides in to divert the ball into the bottom-right corner.

17 April 2005

United's last chance of silverware for the season is on the line against Newcastle United in the FA Cup semi-final at the Millennium Stadium. After a largely disappointing campaign, the Reds target the oldest knockout trophy in the world and take the lead when Cristiano Ronaldo's low cross from the right is just about turned into the bottom-left corner of the net by Ruud van Nistelrooy – his first in nine games – to make it 1-0.

20 August 2006

Punch-drunk Fulham's nightmare start to the 2006/07 season gets worse as United score a fourth goal inside the opening 20 minutes. The first three goals had come from crosses from either flank and the fourth is no different as Wayne Rooney checks inside on to his right foot before sending an inch-perfect cross in from the left flank for Cristiano Ronaldo to race on to and half-volley into the roof of the net from the corner of the six-yard box.

10 April 2007

Rampant United go 3-0 up against Roma with less than 20 minutes played. The Italians are stunned by the Reds' ferocious start and can't live with the movement and trickery and when Ryan Giggs bursts down the right flank, his low cross is met with a deft flick by Rooney to put United firmly on course for the Champions League semi-finals – though there is much more to come.

29 October 2011

United get back to basics in order to wipe out the memory of losing 6-1 at Old Trafford to Manchester City the week before. In what will be a watertight defensive display away to Everton, Javier Hernandez taps home from two yards following an excellent cross from the left by Patrice Evra. It is enough to give the Reds a 1-0 victory at Goodison Park and a much-needed clean sheet.

29 February 2017

United go ahead in the 2017 League Cup Final against Southampton. The Saints had seen what looked like a perfectly good goal disallowed for offside, and then are punished when a free kick is conceded on the edge of their own box. Zlatan Ibrahimovic steps up to take the kick and curls a shot over the wall and into the left of the net to make it 1-0 for José Mourinho's men.

20

18 December 1999

Ryan Giggs puts United 3-0 up away to West Ham with a superb volley. Dwight Yorke twists one way then the other in the Hammers' box before seeing his shot blocked – but the ball goes straight to Giggs who thumps a 25-yard volley past Shaka Hislop and into the net as the Reds' blistering start rocks the home side. Chants of 'what a load of rubbish' soon follow.

13 May 2011

On an afternoon of high drama and heartache, United take the lead away to Sunderland on the final day of the 2011/12 campaign. United went into the game knowing that if Manchester City – who were playing at home to QPR – should draw or lose and the Reds win, it would be United who would be crowned champions. Wayne Rooney keeps the Reds' side of the bargain as he grabs what will be the only goal of the game at the Stadium of Light. And it looks like it might be enough to stop City winning a first top-flight title in 44 years, with news coming from the Etihad that QPR led 2-1 going into added time, only for City to score twice in the closing seconds and snatch the title away.

13 February 2013

United withstand early pressure to score a crucial away goal in the Champions League round of 16 clash with Real Madrid. It comes from a set-piece as Wayne Rooney's corner sees Danny Welbeck lose the attentions of Sergio Ramos to angle a header past Lopez and silence the majority of the Bernabéu in the process.

20 December 2020

United go 3-0 up against Leeds at Old Trafford as the visitors' poor defending continues. Fred drives forwards before finding Anthony Martial in the box – he has the ball nicked off his toes by Luke Ayling but only as far as Bruno Fernandes who hits a low, angled shot across the keeper and into the bottom-left corner of the net.

21

3 May 1993

Ryan Giggs scores a wonder goal to level the scores with Blackburn Rovers at Old Trafford. Newly crowned champions United had fallen behind to an early Kevin Gallagher goal, but when a free kick is awarded some 25 yards out, Giggs steps up to send a left-footed howitzer arrowing into the top-left corner to make it 1-1.

21 October 1998

A second goal for Ryan Giggs as United go 2-0 up away to Brondby in the Champions League. It's a cracking effort, too, as Jesper Blomqvist crosses in from the left and, timing his run to perfection, Giggs soars to head the ball in just under the crossbar.

16 March 2013

United go 15 points clear at the top of the Premier League thanks to Wayne Rooney's 13th goal in 17 matches. Up against a managerless Reading, Rooney settles a dull game when Rio Ferdinand bursts past three Reading players before laying the ball off to the striker, who sees his shot hit Alex Pearce and loop up and over the keeper to score what will be the only goal of the contest at Old Trafford.

22

24 April 1909

A major moment in the history of Manchester United Football Club as Sandy Turnbull puts the team ahead in their first FA Cup Final. The match is played at Crystal Palace in London in front of 71,401 fans and the only goal of the game comes midway through the first half. A hopeful drive from Harold Halse hits the crossbar and the ball falls to former Manchester City star Turnbull, who fires a shot past goalkeeper Harry Clay to score and win the trophy for United for the first time.

14 August 1994

Paul Ince is brought down in the box by former Manchester City defender Colin Hendry in the FA Charity Shield against Blackburn Rovers. Eric Cantona steps up to take the spot-kick and he comfortably sends keeper Tim Flowers the wrong way to make it 1-0 at Wembley.

25 February 2001

A superb David Beckham pass ends with United going 3-1 up in a breathless start against Arsenal at Old Trafford. Beckham, on the right flank at the halfway line, lofts a 40-yard pass to the accelerating Yorke, who brings the ball down with his chest as he enters the box where he then buries a low shot past Arsenal keeper David Seaman to complete an 18-minute hat-trick.

28 August 2011

Considering what was to follow, it was amazing this Premier League game against Arsenal was still 0-0 a quarter of the way through. But the goals start flowing when Anderson weighs up his options on the edge of the box before scooping a pass over the line of defenders for Danny Welbeck to chase and he holds off two challenges to nod past Wojciech Szczesny from a couple of yards out.

22 April 2013

Surely one of the finest goals Old Trafford has ever witnessed – and on the day a victory will confirm a 20th top-flight title. With United already leading 1-0, Wayne Rooney plays a majestic 50-yard pass from inside his own half into the path of Robin van Persie and as it falls on to his left foot he lashes a volley from 20 yards that rockets past the keeper and into the net. In fact, the ball didn't touch the grass once after leaving Rooney's boot – an incredible goal and one that puts the Reds 2-0 up against Aston Villa.

23

6 May 1967

Thousands of United fans inside Upton Park start the celebrations early as the Reds take an unassailable 4-0 lead midway through the first half of a game that only a point is needed from to be crowned First Division champions. This time, it's George Best who does the damage with a typically nonchalant finish to effectively end the contest with more than two-thirds of the game still remaining! It is the Northern Irishman's tenth of the season.

20 August 1983

At a packed Wembley Stadium and in front of 92,000 sun-drenched fans, United go 1-0 up against Liverpool in the FA Charity Shield. It's a classic goal, too, as a forward ball finds Frank Stapleton just inside the Liverpool half and he flicks it to Ray Wilkins who immediately sets skipper Bryan Robson clear. Robson takes the ball around Ray Clemence on the edge of the box before stroking the ball home from 15 yards.

4 January 1998

David Beckham puts United 1-0 up at Stamford Bridge in the FA Cup third round. The goal is mainly down to Andy Cole, who chases a ball into the box and holds off a challenge before twisting and sending a deflected cross in that Teddy Sheringham flicks on, and Beckham arrives to volley home from six yards out.

16 April 2003

In a crucial title clash between United and Arsenal, the Reds draw first blood at Highbury with a goal that has class stamped all over it. Ruud van Nistelrooy receives a ball down the left flank, just inside the Gunners' half, then lays it back to Ryan Giggs who immediately plays it back to the Dutch striker. He nutmegs Sol Campbell before angling into the box and lifting the ball over the keeper to make it 1-0.

27 November 2010

A proverbial bus could be driven through the Blackburn Rovers defence as United go 2-0 up at Old Trafford. It's all too easy for the Reds as Ji-Sung Park plays a short pass to Wayne Rooney on the edge of the box before running unchallenged on to Rooney's return ball and still having time to place a slow shot past the keeper. Awful defending from Rovers, who will suffer the consequences as the game goes on.

11 May 2011

United's blistering start against Chelsea continues with a second goal in a crucial Premier League title decider at Old Trafford. Ji-Sung Park – outstanding from the kick-off – finds Ryan Giggs on the left of the Chelsea box and skips past a challenge before crossing into the middle where Nemanja Vidic powers a header past Petr Cech to make it 2-0. It will be enough to ensure victory, with the Reds going on to win 2-1 and moving to within one point of being crowned champions with two games remaining.

17 October 2020

United level at 1-1 away to Newcastle. The Reds had trailed after a second-minute Luke Shaw own goal had given the hosts the lead – and saw a spectacular Bruno Fernandes strike ruled out by VAR – before skipper Harry Maguire rises to head a Juan Mata corner across the keeper and into the bottom-right-hand corner. It was a superb goal from the Reds defender.

24

11 August 1996

United go ahead against Newcastle in the FA Charity Shield. Eric Cantona had already missed two good chances when the Reds win the ball just inside the Magpies half. David Beckham takes the play on and finds Cantona in space on the right and the French striker calmly strokes a shot past the keeper to make it 1-0 at Wembley.

21 April 1999

Stunned by two Juventus goals in the first 11 minutes, United keep their nerve and pull one back in Turin to make the aggregate score 3-2 in the Italians' favour. Typically, skipper Roy Keane leads from the front as he glances home David Beckham's near-post corner to head across the keeper and into the far corner of the net.

1 April 2000

Paul Scholes levels for United against West Ham at Old Trafford. The visitors had taken a surprise lead through Paulo Wanchope, but the Premier League leaders strike back when Quinton Fortune's cross is only cleared as far as Scholes on the edge of the box and his low shot through a crowded area finds the bottom-left corner to make it 1-1 at Old Trafford.

6 April 2011

United get a vital away goal to take command of the Champions League quarter-final against Chelsea at Stamford Bridge. Michael Carrick sprays a superb, lofted pass out to Ryan Giggs, whose sublime control and touch sees him drift past the left-back before pulling a low ball back into the middle for Wayne Rooney who side-foots a measured shot in off the foot of the right-hand post to put the Reds 1-0 up – it will be the only goal of the first leg in west London.

10 March 2018

United again profit from a long David de Gea goal kick to double the lead against Liverpool at Old Trafford. The Spaniard – who combined with Romelu Lukaku to set up Marcus Rashford's opening goal – picks out the Belgian once more and this time he brings the ball down and plays Juan Mata into the box. When Mata's effort is saved, Rashford buries a low shot past the keeper into the bottom-right corner to put the Reds 2-0 up.

21 April 2018

United level at Wembley against Tottenham Hotspur in the FA Cup semi-final. Spurs – who played all their home games at Wembley during 2017/18 while their new stadium was being built – had gone ahead on 11 minutes through Dele Alli, but the Reds don't take too much time to level. Moussa Dembele receives a pass on the left of his own box but tries to cut inside Paul Pogba, who dispossess him before delivering a superb cross towards the back post where Alexis Sanchez heads back across the keeper and into the far corner to make it 1-1.

25

29 August 1908

Former Manchester City star Billy Meredith and Jimmy Turnbull combine to put United 1-0 up in the FA Charity Shield replay at Stamford Bridge. Watched on by a crowd of 50,000, it is the Reds who strike first against QPR on what will be a memorable day for Scottish forward Turnbull, who heads home his first of the afternoon from a Meredith cross.

26 May 1983

United open the scoring in the 1983 FA Cup Final replay. The first game had ended 2-2 at Wembley five days before, but the general feeling was that Brighton & Hove Albion had missed their chance to win the trophy and when Alan Davies lays off a ball to Bryan Robson on the edge of the box, the United captain hits a superb, angled left-foot shot low into the bottom-right corner to make it 1-0.

25 November 1998

Despite falling behind to Barcelona in the first minute in the Champions League group stage match at the Camp Nou, United fight back to level the scores when Jesper Blomqvist plays a pass in from the left to Dwight Yorke. Yorke drives towards the edge of the box before hitting a low shot into the bottom-left corner to make it 1-1.

16 September 1998

Dwight Yorke is denied a wonder strike by the Barcelona keeper as he acrobatically sends an overhead volley goalwards from six yards out – but Barca's respite lasts for milliseconds and Paul Scholes sweeps home the rebound to put the Reds 2-0 up in the opening Champions League group stage clash at Old Trafford.

23 November 2002

Paul Scholes opens the scoring against Newcastle at Old Trafford but it is Ole Gunnar Solskjaer who makes the goal. The Norwegian, out on the right flank, manages to control a high pass and as he brings the ball down, he slips it through the full-back's legs as he heads to the corner of the Magpies' box. Solskjaer just gets there before another challenge comes in and slips a low cross into the middle where Scholes arrives on cue to thunder a shot into the top-right corner from eight yards out.

2 February 2021

United double the lead against ten-man Southampton at Old Trafford. Luke Shaw assisted the first goal against his old club and he plays a major role in the second as he drives into the box before finding Mason Greenwood to his left. Greenwood picks out Marcus Rashford on the penalty spot from where his low, right-footed volley beats the keeper's poor attempt at a save to make it 2-0.

19 March 2014

Trailing 2-0 to Olympiakos from the first leg of their Champions League round of 16 tie, United get the breakthrough in the second leg when the referee awards a penalty. Wayne Rooney sends a superb pass to the chest of Robin van Persie who is clattered from behind by José Holebas as he controls the ball, giving the official an easy decision. Van Persie keeps his cool as the Greeks protest and though the keeper guesses the right way, he can't stop the shot as the Dutchman makes it 1-0 on the night and halves the deficit overall.

26

25 February 2001

An on-fire Dwight Yorke adds an assist to his hat-trick as United go 4-1 up against title rivals Arsenal at Old Trafford. Yorke wriggles past a challenge and races down the left flank before picking out the run of Roy Keane through the middle and the skipper takes one touch before hitting a low shot past David Seaman into the bottom-left corner.

21 May 2008

United take the lead against Chelsea in the 2008 Champions League Final. The game, played at the Luzhniki Stadium in Moscow, sees the all-Premier League occasion have a cagey first 20 minutes or so with few chances, but when Wes Brown has time on the right he sends a cross into the box where Cristiano Ronaldo leaps to head inside the left post to put the Reds 1-0 up.

27

7 February 1970

George Best was not expected to feature in the FA Cup fifth-round tie away to Northampton Town having been out of the side while serving a four-week ban for knocking the ball from referee Jack Taylor's hands at the end of a Manchester derby. The mercurial Northern Irishman soon made up for lost time against the Cobblers in what would be an unforgettable individual performance that started when he rose to head the ball home from eight yards to put the Reds 1-0 up at the County Ground.

4 December 1999

Denis Irwin scores from the penalty spot to level against Everton in a bright and breezy first half at Old Trafford. Everton had gone ahead on eight minutes through Francis Jeffers, but when future Manchester City skipper Richard Dunne handles a cross from the right, the ref points to the spot and Irwin converts his second goal of the season to make it 1-1.

1 April 2000

United are awarded a penalty as Roy Keane goes down in the box under a tackle from West Ham's Steve Potts. The Hammers defender insists Keane dived and TV replays suggest there wasn't much contact as he burst into the box after a one-two with Dwight Yorke, but the decision stands and Denis Irwin steps up. Keeper Craig Forrest guesses right and saves his spot-kick but can only push it back to Irwin, who makes no mistake with the rebound.

27 November 2010

United have the points as good as wrapped up with only 27 minutes gone as Dimitar Berbatov scores his second – and the Reds' third – against a woeful Blackburn Rovers. Pascal Chimbonda doesn't even look as he plays an under-hit pass back towards his keeper and the lurking Berbatov says 'thank you very much' as he intercepts and is able to stroll a few yards into the box before firing a powerful, rising shot past Paul Robinson to make it 3-0.

12 April 2015

With City's title defence in tatters, United rub salt in the wounds as Marouane Fellaini makes it 2-1 at Old Trafford. Ashley Young, who had levelled the scores on 14 minutes, is the provider on this occasion, curling in a beauty of a cross towards the back post where Fellaini heads home powerfully with the Blues' defence at sixes and sevens.

28

24 April 1948

Appearing in a first FA Cup Final for exactly 39 years, United equalise against Blackpool in front of a Wembley crowd of 99,842. Eddie Shimwell had put the Tangerines ahead from the penalty spot after Stan Mortensen had been tripped but Jack Rowley levels for the Reds, who were wearing navy blue and white, as he knocks the ball over Seasiders keeper Joe Robinson before walking it into the net to make it 1-1.

15 August 1965

A classic FA Charity Shield clash between United and Liverpool at Old Trafford, watched by almost 50,000, ignites when George Best puts the Reds ahead. With Matt Busby and Bill Shankly trying to outwit one another, it is the Northern Irish superstar who shakes off the attentions of two Liverpool defenders before burying a low shot past Liverpool keeper Tommy Lawrence.

4 January 1998

United go 2-0 up against Chelsea with a David Beckham special. The England midfielder had already put the Reds ahead six minutes earlier when a free kick was awarded 25 yards out. Spotting gaps around the Chelsea wall, Beckham curls his shot into the bottom-right corner to put United in command at Stamford Bridge. TV replays show Mark Hughes drag a Chelsea player on the end of the wall out of the way – VAR would definitely have chalked off the goal today.

21 October 1998

Andy Cole gets in on the act as United go 3-0 up against Brondby. The Danish champions are left reeling as Cole chests the ball down outside the box and beats a defender before driving home a precise, low shot into the bottom-right corner to put the Reds in total control of the Champions League group stage match.

4 November 1998

Another howler from the hapless Brondby keeper sees United go 4-0 up with less than half an hour played. David Beckham's right-wing cross finds the head of Dwight Yorke, who heads powerfully down and the keeper allows the ball to squirm underneath his body as the visitors – who lost the first group stage fixture 6-2 – concede a tenth goal in approximately two hours of Champions League football against the Reds.

18 December 2008

In the semi-final of the FIFA Club World Cup, United take the lead against Gamba Osaka in Tokyo. The Reds take what is a deserved lead when Ryan Giggs sends in a corner and Nemanja Vidic climbs higher than Osaka skipper Yamaguchi to head home with keeper Fujigaya hopelessly stranded.

28 August 2011

United go 2-0 up against Arsenal at Old Trafford. Wayne Rooney bursts down the left flank but his low cross into the box is cleared, only as far as Ashley Young, who takes a touch to tee himself up before curling a beautiful shot into the top-right corner from 25 yards out. A stunning strike.

29

8 April 1990

Bryan Robson brings United level in the FA Cup semi-final derby with Oldham Athletic at Maine Road. The Latics had led from the fifth minute when former Manchester City player Earl Barrett opened the scoring from close range, but Robson equalises just before the half-hour as he races on to a fine Neil Webb through ball to hit a low drive that the keeper gets a hand to but can't prevent trickling into the bottom-left corner to make it 1-1.

4 December 1999

Ole Gunnar Solskjaer makes it two goals in three minutes as United come from behind to lead 2-1 against Everton at Old Trafford. Paul Scholes sends a superb through ball for the Norwegian striker to run on to and though his shot is partially saved by keeper Paul Gerrard, its momentum carries the ball over the line to put the Reds ahead.

1 November 2008

United re-take the lead against Hull City at Old Trafford. The visitors had equalised Cristiano Ronaldo's early strike but fall behind again when Dimitar Berbatov carries the ball towards their box before playing it left to Michael Carrick who hits a crisp, angled left-footed drive in off the foot of the right post to give the Reds a 2-1 lead.

9 December 2012

United double their lead over City at the Etihad as Wayne Rooney becomes the leading scorer in Manchester derbies. Antonio Valencia passes to the overlapping Rafael and his low cross from the right finds Rooney in space. His low shot into the bottom-left corner after going through a City defender's legs – just as his first 13 minutes earlier had – makes it 2-0 for the Reds.

30

29 August 1908

Jimmy Turnbull makes it two goals in five minutes to put United 2-0 up against QPR in the FA Charity Shield replay at Stamford Bridge. Jack Picken's burst into the box looks set to be foiled by keeper Charlie Shaw, who races out – but he slips as he does so, leaving Turnbull with the simple task of rolling the ball into the empty net.

25 May 1963

Denis Law gives United the lead in the FA Cup Final at Wembley with a typical poacher's goal against Leicester City. The Foxes had been marginally the better side for the opening half-hour, but the Reds finally take change when Paddy Crerand intercepts a clearance and crosses low into the box where Law, with his back to goal, takes one touch before turning and hitting a low shot into the bottom-right corner to make it 1-0.

26 May 1983

Alan Davies, after setting up the opening goal against Brighton & Hove Albion just five minutes earlier, is again the creator as United take a commanding 2-0 lead. The Welsh midfielder is first to a partially cleared ball on the left of the Seagulls' box and he looks up before sending a delightful, chipped cross into the middle for Norman

Whiteside to meet with a fine header into the bottom-right corner.

11 August 1996

Nicky Butt powers a header home to put United 2-0 up against Newcastle in the FA Charity Shield. Ryan Giggs sprays a ball out to the right where Eric Cantona cheekily back-flicks to David Beckham and the England midfielder drills a superb cross into the box that a flying Butt meets full on to give the Magpies keeper no chance whatsoever.

30 September 1998

United level away to Bayern Munich in the second Champions League group stage match of the 1998/99 campaign. David Beckham attacks down the right wing before just managing to whip a cross in to the middle where Dwight Yorke dives to head home at the far post and make it 1-1 in Munich.

22 April 2000

Ole Gunnar Solskjaer scores the third goal of a scintillating first half-hour away to Southampton. The Reds go 3-0 up when David Beckham plays a superb, angled chip from the right into the path of Solskjaer who chests the ball down before firing a shot across the keeper and into the bottom-right corner of the net to ensure United win a sixth Premier League title in eight years – and with four games still to go before the end of the season.

21 October 2008

Dimitar Berbatov puts United ahead against Celtic in a Champions League group stage clash at Old Trafford. In front of almost 75,000 fans, the Reds strike first as a corner is eventually jabbed forward by John O'Shea to the Bulgarian striker on the edge of the six-yard box and his clever flick gives the keeper no chance. The Celtic players' claims for offside are waved away by the referee who might have thought a Celtic defender actually got a foot to the ball first.

13 September 2006

In a Champions League group stage clash (predictably) dubbed 'The Battle of Britain', Ryan Giggs wins United a penalty against Celtic. Trailing 1-0 to the Scottish champions, Giggs chases Paul Scholes's long ball and as he enters the box, keeper Artur Boruc brushes against the Welshman who then goes down. It is a harsh decision to award the spot-kick, but Louis Saha isn't worried and proves as much as he tucks the ball into the bottom-left corner to make it 1-1.

8 January 2012

United double the lead against ten-man Manchester City at the Etihad with a superb piece of improvisation by Danny Welbeck. Nani's trickery on the edge of the box allows Patrice Evra to run into space on the left of the box and his low cross sees two partial attempts by City defenders to clear but the ball flips up near the penalty spot and Welbeck adjusts to spin and volley a shot into the bottom-right corner and make it 2-0 in the FA Cup third round tie.

19 May 2013

United are in cruise control as Alexander Buttner makes it 3-0 at The Hawthorns on the final day of the 2012/13 season. Already crowned Premier League champions, the Reds look set to mark Sir Alex Ferguson's final game in charge with a landslide win over West Brom as Tom Cleverley, on the edge of the box, plays the ball to his left and Buttner drills an angled shot into the bottom-right corner.

6 March 2019

Trailing 3-1 on aggregate in the Champions League round of 16 second leg, United take a 2-1 lead over Paris St Germain with only a half hour played. Marcus Rashford's shot from distance is fumbled by Italy legend Gianluigi Buffon and Romelu Lukaku is quickest to react and finishes from close range.

8 March 2020

United take the lead in the Manchester derby at Old Trafford. City, 25 points behind Liverpool but with two games in hand, are already resigned to not being able to retain their championship – but the Reds fans are keen to rub salt in the wounds, even at the expense of Liverpool winning a first Premier League title. Bruno Fernandes goes down under the challenge of Ilkay Gundogan 35 yards from goal. Fernandes then dinks the ball over the City defensive line for Anthony Martial to volley a low shot that squirms beneath Ederson's body and into the net to put United – who desperately need victory to maintain a push for a Champions League berth – 1-0 up against Pep Guardiola's men.

31

3 April 2004

Paul Scholes ends Arsenal's hopes of the treble and a third successive FA Cup triumph with a first-half winner against the Gunners in the semi-final at Villa Park. The title was almost certainly headed to Highbury with Arsenal unbeaten in all their Premier League games, but the Reds are desperate to stop Arsène Wenger's men having it all their own way and when Scholes fires home Ryan Giggs's cross from close range, United book a place in the final against either Sunderland or Millwall.

32

12 April 2003

United begin a devastating 26-minute spell at St James'
Park during which six goals are scored. Needing to
win to go three points clear of Arsenal at the top of
the Premier League, the Reds initially fall behind to
Newcastle thanks to a Jermaine Jenas wonder strike.
But they respond with Ruud van Nistelrooy finding
Ryan Giggs on the left and the winger checks back on
the corner of the Magpies' box before crossing into the
middle where Ole Gunnar Solskjaer has timed his run
to perfection, beats the offside trap and has time to
bring the ball down before putting it past the keeper
from a few yards out to make it 1-1.

3 May 2003

United re-take the lead against Charlton Athletic at Old
Trafford. The visitors had levelled after a mistake by
keeper Roy Carroll in a game the Reds must win to stay
in control of the title race – as well as piling pressure
on the chasing Arsenal – but when David Beckham's
corner is knocked down, Ruud van Nistelrooy spins in
the six-yard box and rifles the ball home to make it 2-1.
It is his 41st goal of the season and also the ninth game
in succession the Dutch striker has scored in.

7 August 2016

Jesse Lingard's superb individual goal gives United a 1-0 lead in the FA Community Shield clash with Leicester City. When Lingard receives the ball some 40 yards from goal, there is anything but a clear path ahead of him, but he wriggles between a couple of challenges before moving past a couple more and keeps going into the box before placing a low shot past Kasper Schmeichel to put the Reds ahead.

33

26 February 2006

Wayne Rooney puts United ahead in the League Cup Final against Wigan Athletic at the Millennium Stadium. Rooney tries to burst past two Wigan defenders who collide with one another before collecting the loose ball and lashes a shot over sub keeper John Filan as he races off his line from 15 yards out.

22 April 2013

Robin van Persie completes a 31-minute hat-trick to put United 3-0 up against Aston Villa at Old Trafford. His third of the evening is all thanks to the unselfishness of Ryan Giggs who races clear into the box but instead of shooting, he squares the ball to van Persie who takes a touch to take it out of the keeper's reach before thumping a powerful, rising drive in off the left post and into the roof of the net. With no further scoring, United are confirmed as Premier League champions for the 20th time on the final whistle.

22 March 2014

United go 2-0 up at Upton Park with a gift of a goal. Already leading from Wayne Rooney's stunning strike from just inside the West Ham half, the second comes when Ashley Young send a cross into the six-yard box and home skipper Mark Noble inexplicably knocks the ball back across goal and straight to Rooney who finishes with ease from a few yards out. It is a strike that puts the United forward into third position in the Reds' all-time top scorers' chart with 212 goals and counting.

34

21 April 1999

How a Champions League semi-final second leg can turn in the space of ten minutes! The Reds had trailed 2-0 to two early Juventus goals but Dwight Yorke makes it 2-2 when he heads home Andy Cole's clever cross from the right to suddenly put United in the box seat and, as things stood, ahead on away goals.

22 December 2001

Despite the presence of seven defenders in or around the six-yard box, Southampton fail to clear a cross into the box and as the ball bobbles around, it falls to the predatory Ruud van Nistelrooy, who spins and manages to hit the ball past the keeper from a couple of yards out for his second of the game to put the Reds 2-0 up.

12 April 2003

United go 2-1 up with a second goal in three minutes away to Newcastle. The title-chasing Reds are at their devastating best as a smart exchange of passes eventually sees Paul Scholes play a ball into the feet of Ole Gunnar Solskjaer on the edge of the Magpies' box and then run on to the Norwegian's looped return pass before volleying a low shot past Shay Given from 12 yards.

14 February 2004

United go 1-0 up against Manchester City in the FA Cup fifth round derby at Old Trafford. The opener comes as Ruud van Nistelrooy feeds the ball wide to the left for Ryan Giggs and his superb low cross into the six-yard box is turned home by Paul Scholes, who had managed to get between two defenders and side-foot home from close range.

5 May 2007

The scenario no Manchester City fan wanted – United winning the title at the Etihad – doesn't quite happen on the day but this 1-0 victory will be enough to ensure Chelsea won't catch the Reds.

The only goal of the game comes when Michael Ball fouls Cristiano Ronaldo in the box and the referee points to the spot. Ronaldo steps up to take the spot-kick and makes no mistake.

28 May 2011

Wayne Rooney equalises against Barcelona in the 2011 Champions League Final at Wembley. It's a magnificent response by the Reds, who had fallen behind to Pep Guardiola's side just seven minutes earlier as Pedro drilled a low shot past Edwin van der Sar. But United level as Rooney drives forward, finds Ryan Giggs in the box and then runs on to the Welshman's return, sweeping a right-footed drive into the top-left corner to make it 1-1. However, it will not be United's night, with second-half goals from Lionel Messi and David Villa securing the Catalans' victory.

23 April 2016

Marouane Fellaini puts United 1-0 up against former club Everton. The FA Cup semi-final at Wembley had passed with little threat on the Toffees' goal until Anthony Martial weaves into the left of the box before picking out Fellaini near the penalty spot and the Belgian plants a left-footed shot into the right corner of the net to give the Reds the edge.

2 February 2021

Comical defending by ten-man Southampton results in United going 3-0 up at Old Trafford. Three Saints defenders contrive to work a poor clearance to the right flank where Marcus Rashford fires a dangerous cross into the six-yard box and Jan Bednarek turns the ball past his own keeper – though in fairness either of the two United players behind him would almost certainly have scored anyway – to almost end the game as a contest with only 34 minutes on the clock.

35

12 May 1990

United equalise against Steve Coppell's Crystal Palace in the 1990 FA Cup Final. The Reds had fallen behind to an early set-piece goal for the Eagles but work a way back into the game when Brian McClair and Danny Wallace exchange passes on the right of the Palace box and McClair crosses towards the back post where skipper Bryan Robson heads down powerfully into the bottom-left corner with the help of a slight deflection to make it 1-1.

30 November 1999

United compete in the Intercontinental Cup – a clash between the winners of the 1998/99 Champions League, and Brazilian side Palmeiras, winners of the 1999 Copa Libertadores. In the National Stadium, Tokyo, the Reds score the only goal of the game as a lovely sweeping move sees Ryan Giggs race down the left flank before sending in a deep cross that sails over the keeper and Roy Keane, arriving at the back post, is on hand to volley the ball home from close range.

5 August 2007

Ryan Giggs puts United ahead in the FA Community Shield at Wembley. Nemanja Vidic finds Patrice Evra on the left with a fine crossfield pass and Evra exchanges passes with Cristiano Ronaldo before teeing up Giggs, who fires a shot into the roof of the net. Chelsea will level through Florent Malouda to force a penalty shoot-out.

29 January 2020

Trailing 3-1 from the League Cup semi-final first leg against Manchester City, United go 1-0 up at the Etihad. A free kick from the left of City's box is half-cleared by the home defence but only as far as Nemanja Matic who hits a crisp, first-time shot into the bottom-right corner from 12 yards to put the Reds very much back in the tie.

36

7 February 1970

George Best scores his second of the afternoon with a delightful piece of skill that puts United 2-0 up away to Northampton Town. Chasing a long ball towards the Cobblers' box, Best's first touch takes him around keeper Kim Book – brother of Manchester City captain Tony Book – before slotting a low shot into the bottom-left corner.

20 September 2017

A forgettable goal? Yes – but United score so rarely in the 36th minute that it gets an unexpected showcasing here. Jesse Lingard's low shot takes a deflection that sends the ball into the opposite corner as the Reds take a 3-0 lead over League One strugglers Burton Albion in the League Cup. Most fans who were at Old Trafford that night will have forgotten it – maybe even Lingard – but it is scored in that rarest of minutes for Manchester United and up to March 2021, there hasn't been one since.

37

4 March 1995

Old Trafford celebrates as United score a fine third goal against Ipswich Town. Andrei Kanchelskis dinks a cross into the middle from the right of the box and Mark Hughes acrobatically thunders an overhead kick against the crossbar but the rebound falls to Andy Cole, who has time to control the ball and then calmly slot into the bottom-right corner for his second of the afternoon and to put the Reds 3-0 up.

30 March 2002

United go back in front against Leeds at Elland Road with a typical poacher's goal from Ole Gunnar Solskjaer. The Reds had taken an early lead before Mark Viduka had levelled for the hosts – but when a mix-up between Danny Mills and Jonathan Woodgate to the left of the Leeds box sees the ball break loose to Ryan Giggs, he immediately feeds Paul Scholes to his right and Scholes takes a touch before firing a low shot from 20 yards. Keeper Nigel Martyn can only parry and Solskjaer is quickest to react, lashing an angled drive past Martyn to put United 2-1 up.

3 May 2003

United increase their lead over Charlton Athletic at Old Trafford to 3-1. The goal has a simple directness about it.

Mikael Silvestre – so effective throughout the 2003/04 campaign with his overlapping runs and crossing ability – sends a ball towards the box from midway on the left. Ole Gunnar Solskjaer flicks the ball on with his head and Ruud van Nistelrooy manages to get the knock-on first then as the keeper comes out, he lifts the ball over his head and into the net for his second of the game and 42nd of a prolific season.

20 December 2020

Victor Lindelof scores United's fourth of the first half thanks to more shocking defending by Leeds. Anthony Martial's near-post flick finds Lindelof completely unmarked in the six-yard box and the Swede finishes confidently from close range.

38

25 February 2001

Ole Gunnar Solskjaer makes it 5-1 for United against Arsenal as the Reds run riot against Arsène Wenger's men. Nicky Butt leaves a defender on his backside before picking out Solskjaer's run towards the six-yard box and his low cross is expertly turned home by the Norwegian.

23 November 2002

United go 2-1 up against Newcastle at Old Trafford. Terrific battling on the left flank by Mikael Silvestre sees him win one challenge, then another, before turning a defender inside out and sending a deep cross into the Newcastle box for Ruud van Nistelrooy to head home from close range and restore United's lead.

12 April 2003

A third goal in a blistering six-minute spell at St James' Park puts United 3-1 up against Newcastle. Ryan Giggs picks up the ball on the left after a short corner and weaves past a few challenges and into the box where he lays it off to Wes Brown, who nudges the ball back to Paul Scholes on the edge of the D and his first-time howitzer of a shot arrows into the top-right corner. It's United at their very best and the shell-shocked Magpies can barely believe they were 1-0 up just seven minutes earlier.

14 February 2004

Gary Neville is shown a red card after an altercation in the FA Cup fifth round against Manchester City. The incident, which has a strong Merseyside influence, sees Neville make the most of a challenge from City's Michael Tarnat and when referee Jeff Winter doesn't award a penalty, Neville beats the ground in frustration causing an angry reaction from City players who felt he'd dived. Former Liverpool winger Steve McManaman makes his feelings known and Neville reacts when the pair move their heads close together with what looks like a headbutt attempt. Joey Barton and Robbie Fowler get involved, as do most of the players, but Neville is ordered off by the ref for an early bath.

29 February 2017

A very cool finish from Jesse Lingard puts United 2-0 up in the League Cup Final against Southampton at Wembley. Marcos Rojo attacks from the left of Saints' area before sliding a ball to Lingard on the edge of the box where he takes one touch to tee himself up before calmly passing the ball past keeper Fraser Forster and into the bottom-right corner of the net.

39

30 March 2002

Ole Gunnar Solskjaer scores his second goal in three minutes to put United 3-1 up against Leeds at Elland Road. Paul Scholes – involved in both of the Reds' first two goals – plays a clever ball down the left for Mikael Silvestre, who cuts a low cross back into the middle where Ryan Giggs's effort is blocked and Solskjaer follows up with a low shot that beats the keeper and increases United's lead.

2 February 2021

Luke Shaw claims his second assist of the game as United go 4-0 up against ten-man Southampton at Old Trafford. It's as simple as you like, too, as Shaw, with time and space on the left of the box, is able to pick out Edinson Cavani around the penalty spot and the Uruguayan thunders a header into the bottom-left corner.

40

13 September 2006

United come from behind to lead 2-1 against Celtic in a lively Champions League group stage clash at Old Trafford. Paul Scholes threads a superb pass into the box for Louis Saha, who tucks a low shot past Artur Boruc, and though the keeper gets something on it, the ball trickles inside the post.

8 January 2012

United fans are in dreamland as Wayne Rooney makes it 3-0 against Manchester City at the Etihad. The Reds had suffered a humiliating 6-1 defeat at Old Trafford just ten weeks earlier and were desperate to put one over on the Blues who were also now Premier League title rivals. With City reduced to ten men following Vincent Kompany's 12th-minute dismissal, the Reds are given the chance to go in at the break with a 3-0 lead and a possibility of erasing that 6-1 loss with a sizeable victory on City's turf. Danny Welbeck is brought down in the box by Aleksandar Kolarov and the referee points to the spot. Rooney steps up and sees his penalty well saved by City keeper Costel Pantilimon, but he can only push the ball up and Rooney races in to head home his second of the game. United are pegged back after the break and will eventually edge into the fourth round with a 3-2 win.

41

22 December 2001

It's all too easy for United, who go 3-0 up just before the break against a poor Southampton side. The third goal is simplicity itself as Nicky Butt's corner is met on the volley by Ole Gunnar Solskjaer, who steers his shot past Paul Jones to virtually wrap the points up.

7 April 2010

United seem on course for a big victory over Bayern Munich as Nani hammers home their third of the first half in the Champions League quarter-final second leg at Old Trafford. Antonio Valencia's low cross into the box is missed by Wayne Rooney but is struck with venom as it goes through to the unmarked Nani, who gives the keeper no chance with a rising shot from 15 yards. It puts United 4-2 up on aggregate against the serial Bundesliga winners and motoring towards the semi-finals – but a comeback by Bayern, who score twice to stun the home fans already reeling from Rafael Da Silva's dismissal, will eventually see the Germans progress on the away goals rule.

8 August 2010

Antonio Valencia puts United 1-0 up against Chelsea in the FA Community Shield at Wembley. Chelsea had gone close on at least two occasions before the Reds take the lead with Antonio Valencia running on to Wayne Rooney's cut-back to hammer a shot into the roof of the net from eight yards.

28 August 2011

Arsenal's miserable first half at Old Trafford gets worse as they concede a third just before the break. When Ashley Young is hauled down outside the box, Wayne Rooney steps up to curl a 20-yard shot into the top-left corner to put the Reds 3-0 up and on course for a big win.

42

30 November 2008

United finally break the deadlock at the Etihad as Wayne Rooney scores his 100th goal for the club. And what a stage to do it – in the Manchester derby on the turf of your fiercest rivals with what will prove the match-winning strike coming just before the break as City fail to clear the danger and Michael Carrick drills a low shot that Joe Hart can only parry into the path of Rooney, who slots the ball home to make it 1-0.

43

17 April 1971

Denis Law sparks a United comeback that will spawn five goals in 23 minutes away to Crystal Palace. Trailing 2-0 to the Eagles, Law receives the ball on the edge of the box before playing a clever pass to Alan Gowling, who takes it into the box before squaring it into the middle where Law nips in to flick the ball home from close range and halve the deficit.

9 December 1998

Roy Keane drills home a crucial opening goal against Bayern Munich in a Champions League group stage clash to decide the group winners. Ryan Giggs is the architect, jinking past a challenge on the left before playing a precise pass to the edge of the box where Keane sweeps home into the bottom-left corner to make it 1-0 at Old Trafford.

4 December 1999

Ole Gunnar Solskjaer scores his second goal of the game to put United 3-1 up against Everton at Old Trafford. The Reds' third is similar to the second in that Paul Scholes again puts the Norwegian striker clear and his shot has just enough to beat the keeper as it bobbles over the line.

12 April 2011

Superb play by Ryan Giggs puts United 1-0 up just before the break in the Champions League quarter-final second leg against Chelsea. The veteran winger gets into the Chelsea box as he beats his man on the right before playing an inch-perfect low cross to Javier Hernandez, who slides in at the far post to fire the ball into the roof of the net and put the Reds 2-0 up on aggregate at Old Trafford.

26 September 2020

United equalise just three minutes after falling behind to Brighton & Hove Albion. Neal Maupay's penalty had given the Seagulls the lead but when a free kick is awarded to the Reds on the left of the Brighton box, Bruno Fernandes finds Nemanja Matic at the far post and his deft volley back into the six-yard box is deflected into the net by Lewis Dunk (with Harry Maguire lurking) to make it 1-1 at the Amex Stadium.

44

26 May 1983

United all but seal victory before half-time in the 1983 FA Cup Final replay. With Brighton rocking on the ropes and just trying to see out the remaining minutes of the first half, a free kick on the left is nodded on by skipper Bryan Robson towards the back post where Frank Stapleton gets up and heads back across the keeper. Robson finishes the job, powering a shot into the roof of the net from about a yard out to make it 3-0 at Wembley.

18 August 1990

United take the lead against Liverpool moments before half-time in the FA Charity Shield. The Reds attack down the right through Mike Phelan and his low cross into the middle is missed by Mark Hughes, Bruce Grobbelaar and a defender, giving Clayton Blackmore the simplest of tap-ins to make it 1-0. The game will end 1-1 and the clubs share the Shield for six months each – the last time this would happen before the format was changed to ensure there was a winner on the day.

28 November 1990

Mark Hughes doubles United's lead against Arsenal. The Reds had gone ahead after just two minutes of the League Cup third round tie at Highbury and score a second just before the break in a sweeping move that starts with Clayton Blackmore feeding Lee Sharpe on the left flank. Sharpe plays it inside to Danny Wallace, who shapes up to take on a defender before playing a short pass to the unmarked Hughes on the edge of the box and the Welsh striker hits a powerful low drive to David Seaman's right to make it 2-0.

12 April 2003

When John O'Shea is delving into his box of tricks, you can be pretty sure United are on the way to a big win. The Reds defender shows his technique on the left flank by forcing the ball through a defender's legs, then dragging it back to go inside another challenge and only the woodwork denies him a memorable goal – but Ryan Giggs is on hand to thump a powerful, angled shot from the rebound to put United 4-1 up away to Newcastle having scored four goals in the space of 12 minutes.

22 May 2004

Cristiano Ronaldo finally breaks Championship side Millwall's stubborn resistance in the FA Cup Final at Cardiff's Millennium Stadium. Millwall, only the second club outside the top flight to reach the final since 1982, manage to keep the Reds at bay until the stroke of half-time when Gary Neville's cross finds the head of Ronaldo at the far post and the Portuguese nods firmly past Andy Marshall to make it 1-0.

10 April 2007

United wrap up victory before half-time with another well-crafted goal against Roma. As the Reds counter attack, Cristiano Ronaldo checks his run to stay onside, receives the ball and heads in from the right towards the box where he catches the keeper off guard with a low, right-footed shot that sneaks in the near post to make it 4-0 on the night and 5-2 on aggregate in the Champions League quarter-final second leg.

1 November 2008

United go 3-1 up against Hull City on the stroke of half-time as Cristiano Ronaldo bags his second of the game. It comes from a set-piece as Nani's outswinging corner finds the leap of Ronaldo and the Portuguese shows his heading ability by powering the ball past the keeper from six yards out.

45

4 January 1998

United ensure the half-time cup of tea and chat is a relaxed one as Andy Cole is set clear on the halfway line. The striker has space and pace as he enters the left side of the box where he fires a rising angled shot over Chelsea keeper Ed de Goey to make it 3-0 in a one-sided FA Cup tie at Stamford Bridge.

3 March 1999

Dwight Yorke's second of the evening puts United 2-0 up against Inter Milan in the Champions League quarter-final first leg – and it's almost a carbon copy of the first goal, with David Beckham's precision right-wing cross finding the head of Yorke in a crowded six-yard box to head down and past the keeper.

11 September 1999

Just when Liverpool defender Jamie Carragher thinks his day can't get any worse – it does. Carragher had headed past his own keeper on four minutes to put United ahead and on the stroke of half-time, he scores his second own goal of the half. In fairness, he knows little about it as a free kick comes into the six-yard box and a game of pinball ensues that sees the ball strike a stumbling Carragher and bounce past the keeper to put the Reds 3-1 up at Anfield.

1 April 2000

Superb play between Dwight Yorke and David Beckham sees Beckham scamper down the right flank before whipping a cross into the middle where Andy Cole rises to direct a fine header past West Ham keeper Craig Forrest to put the Reds 3-1 up on the stroke of half-time in a Premier League match.

17 April 2005

Paul Scholes doubles United's lead on the stroke of half-time in the FA Cup semi-final against Newcastle at the Millennium Stadium. Cristiano Ronaldo's whipped, angled cross from the right allows Scholes to get ahead of the first defender and glance a header into the far left corner of the net, giving keeper Shay Given no chance and putting the Reds firmly in control at 2-0 up.

9 December 2006

Manchester City pay the price of a careless pass as United go 2-0 up on the stroke of half-time at Old Trafford. City had gone behind after just six minutes but largely dominated the rest of the half before a loose pass is intercepted by Wayne Rooney, who finds Gabriel Heinze on the left of the box. Heinze's low cross sees Louis Saha just about get a toe on it and lift it up and over keeper Nicky Weaver and in off the underside of the crossbar.

45+1

23 November 2002

United go 3-1 up against Newcastle on the stroke of half-time. Ryan Giggs sends the impressive Mikael Silvestre scampering away down the left flank and his excellent reverse ball finds the unmarked Diego Forlan on the left corner of the Magpies' box. The Uruguayan hits a low shot towards the six-yard box and Ruud van Nistelrooy turns the ball home from close range.

10 September 2005

United break the deadlock with a goal in first-half stoppage time in the Manchester derby at Old Trafford. When a free kick is awarded in a central position 25 yards out, Paul Scholes elects to fire a direct shot at goal. The power on the strike forces David James to beat the ball out but only as far as Ruud van Nistelrooy, who buries the rebound past James to make it 1-0. TV replays suggest the Dutch striker may have been fractionally offside but the City protests go unheeded by the officials.

18 December 2008

United double the lead in the semi-final of the FIFA Club World Cup in Tokyo. Like the first goal, the second comes from a Ryan Giggs corner as Cristiano Ronaldo rises high to head home unchallenged into the bottom-left corner to make it 2-0 against Gamba Osaka in Tokyo.

5 November 2011

On what is a day of anniversaries and landmarks, Wes Brown scores the only goal of a 1-0 win for United over Sunderland. The only issue for Brown is that he was wearing the red and white stripes of Sunderland when he scores it. On what is Sir Alex Ferguson's 25th anniversary as manager of United – and when it was announced there would be a statue of Ferguson and a stand named after him – Brown deflects the ball past keeper Kieren Westwood after Danny Welbeck had headed on Nani's corner in first-half stoppage time.

19 March 2014

United go 2-0 up against Olympiakos in the Champions League round of 16 second leg at Old Trafford. It also means the aggregate score is level at 2-2 against the Greeks and it is a simple second for Robin van Persie in first-half added time. A searching pass finds Wayne Rooney on the right of the box and though his first touch goes to a Greek defender, he merely deflects it back to the United forward who then sends a low pass to van Persie's feet and he simply side-foots home from six yards.

45+2

28 November 1990

United stun Highbury with a third goal in first-half stoppage time – and what a beauty. With tempers fraying and a few rash challenges going in, Lee Sharpe receives the ball from Colin Gibson and shakes off a nasty tackle from Lee Dixon before teeing himself up to send a curling shot over David Seaman and in off the underside of the crossbar to put the Reds 3-0 up in the League Cup third round tie.

46

30 August 1999

Andy Cole gets his second of the afternoon to put United 2-1 up against Newcastle United at Old Trafford. Paul Scholes sends a long ball towards the Magpies' box where Greek defender Nikos Dabizas gets the flight wrong and Cole nips in to toe-poke the ball around keeper Tommy Wright and into the empty net from eight yards out.

29 September 2001

After receiving the 'hairdryer treatment' from boss Alex Ferguson, United come out for the second half against Tottenham and are barely recognisable from the team that had gone into the break 3-0 down. In the first minute of the second half, Gary Neville crosses in from the right flank and Andy Cole's excellent diving header reduces the deficit in what will be a remarkable 45 minutes for the Reds.

47

15 December 1973

George Best scores the last of his 179 Manchester United goals to level the scores with Coventry City at Old Trafford. United's ageing side will be relegated this season and Best will leave the Reds shortly after, bringing down the curtain on perhaps the most colourful career the club has ever had.

13 September 2006

United regain the lead in the 'Battle of Britain' Champions League group stage clash at Old Trafford. Celtic had levelled just before the break to make it 2-2, but United score two minutes after the re-start as the Hoops again carelessly give possession away to Paul Scholes, who immediately plays a ball into Louis Saha's feet and the French striker sees his shot saved – but he manages to connect with the rebound which sends the ball left to the unmarked Ole Gunnar Solskjaer, who tucks his shot into the unguarded net to put the Reds 3-2 up.

27 November 2010

Dimitar Berbatov starts and finishes a superb move to complete his hat-trick and put United 4-0 up against Blackburn Rovers. Berbatov starts in the Reds' left-back area, exchanging passes with Patrice Evra up to the halfway line before spraying a low, crossfield ball out to Nani on the right. The Portuguese winger moves into the Blackburn box, checks back and threads a low pass to Berbatov who casually thumps it past Paul Robinson from ten yards. Brilliant from the Bulgarian striker.

48

17 April 1971

Denis Law spectacularly levels for United to make it 2-2 at Selhurst Park against Crystal Palace. The Reds had trailed 2-0 before Law pulled one back just before the break – and just after he levels the scores as he meets a cross from the left with an overhead kick that he doesn't quite time right – but it's enough to wrong-foot the keeper and go into the bottom-left corner of the net.

24 May 2017

Henrikh Mkhitaryan puts United 2-0 up against Ajax in the 2017 Europa League Final. Juan Mata sends a ball into the box from the right flank and Chris Smalling climbs to nod the ball down, where Mkhitaryan reacts with an acrobatic volley that rises up and over the keeper and into the roof of the net to put the Reds firmly in control and on the way to another European trophy – a fifth major European honour, in fact.

18 March 2021

Paul Pogba climbs off the bench to score the only goal of the Europa League round of 16, second leg away to AC Milan. Having drawn the first leg 1-1 at Old Trafford, United have to score at the San Siro to have any chance of progressing in the tournament and Pogba – a half-time sub for Marcus Rashford – plants an angled shot past the keeper from close range after a goalmouth scramble. The French midfielder attempts a pass but when the ball comes back to him, he feigns a shot, making the keeper move slightly before he strikes a rising drive into the roof of the net.

49

30 September 1998

Paul Scholes puts United 2-1 up away to Bayern Munich in the Champions League group stage. He chases a ball into the Munich box, causing a defender to mis-hit his clearance and Scholes just keeps going as the keeper fails to collect and even as he attempts to pull him down, the United midfielder manages to knock the loose ball into the net.

10 April 2007

United go 5-0 up against Roma on a horror night for the Serie A side. If there had been any doubts the Reds would progress to the Champions League semi-finals at all, they are swept away as a superb low cross from Ryan Giggs evades Roma defenders and Alan Smith's sliding attempt – but finds Cristiano Ronaldo, who times his run to perfection and finishes from close range for his second of the evening.

11 March 2009

Cristiano Ronaldo scores the all-important second goal to put United 2-0 up against Inter Milan at Old Trafford. Wayne Rooney takes on a defender on the left of the Inter box but catches the defenders cold when he suddenly dinks a cross into the middle where it is met powerfully by the head of Ronaldo to give the keeper no chance whatsoever and ensure the Reds go through to the Champions League quarter-finals.

20 September 2009

United re-take the lead against Manchester City at Old Trafford. United build down the right before the ball is played back to Ryan Giggs, who whips in a high cross towards the six-yard box and Darren Fletcher climbs highest to nod the ball past Shay Given at the back post and put the Reds 2-1 up. It is Fletcher's first goal in almost a year.

50

11 April 1990

Danny Wallace's deflected low cross finds its way to the back post where Brian McClair gleefully taps home to put United 1-0 up in the FA Cup semi-final replay with second-tier Oldham Athletic at Maine Road. However, the Latics, who came back to draw 3-3 in the first clash three days earlier, are not finished yet.

6 February 1999

United go 3-1 up away to Nottingham Forest with a scrappy but welcome goal. After a David Beckham cross is half-cleared by the Forest defence, the ball eventually falls to Dwight Yorke, who fires a low shot that keeper Dave Beasant makes a hash of and Andy Cole is quickest to react, prodding home from close range.

7 March 2021

Luke Shaw puts United 2-0 up against Manchester City after a swift counter-attack doubles the Reds' advantage at the Etihad. City had won their previous 21 games in succession, but when Dean Henderson finds Shaw on the left with a throw-out, the left-back beats Joao Cancelo and powers towards the City box before playing it to Marcus Rashford, who then returns a short pass to Shaw who hits a precise low shot through Rodri's legs and into the bottom-right corner from 15 yards. With no further scoring, it extends United's unbeaten away run to 22 games in all competitions.

51

7 February 1970

George Best completes his hat-trick against Northampton Town to give the Reds a 3-0 lead in the FA Cup fifth-round tie at the County Ground. Brian Kidd bursts down the left flank and into the box before crossing into the six-yard box where a defender's clearance falls to Best, who sees his first shot blocked before rifling home at the second attempt to compete his hat-trick.

21 May 1977

Stuart Pearson puts United ahead in the FA Cup Final with a well-taken goal against Liverpool. Sammy McIlroy knocks the ball on and Jimmy Greenhoff heads it into the path of Pearson, who nods the pass forward before drilling a superb low right-footed shot past Ray Clemence to make it 1-0 at Wembley.

1 April 2000

Rio Ferdinand makes a hash of controlling a long ball into the West Ham half and Andy Cole nips in to steal the ball, immediately playing it to the right of the box for David Beckham. Beckham looks up and sees Paul Scholes well-placed before drilling a low cross that Scholes flicks with his back leg to give Hammers keeper

Craig Forrest no chance and put the Reds 4-1 up at Old Trafford.

21 October 2008

United go 2-0 up against Celtic at Old Trafford in a Champions League group stage clash. The Reds' second of the evening comes when a 25-yard Cristiano Ronaldo free kick is parried by the keeper and Dimitar Berbatov is first to the loose ball, prodding home his second goal from the edge of the six-yard box.

19 March 2014

United finally go ahead overall in the Champions League round of 16 second leg against Greek champions Olympiakos. When the Reds are awarded a free kick, centrally positioned and 25 yards from goal, Robin van Persie and Wayne Rooney stand over the ball. The keeper has clearly decided it will be Rooney to take it, so sets his wall to defend a shot to the right of goal – but Rooney steps over and van Persie hits a left-footed shot over the wall and inside the left post with the keeper taking a fatal step in the wrong direction as the shot is taken. It completes van Persie's hat-trick which had taken just 26 minutes and makes it 3-0 on the night – enough for United to move into the quarter-finals of the competition.

52

4 December 1999

Ole Gunnar Solskjaer completes a 23-minute hat-trick as he puts United 4-1 up against Everton at Old Trafford. Denis Irwin's cross into the box finds the head of Solskjaer, who expertly guides the ball into the bottom-right corner as he again punishes poor Everton defending.

12 April 2003

United make it 5-1 at St James' Park as the dismantling of Newcastle continues. A patient move down the right eventually sees Ole Gunnar Solskjaer play a simple ball to Gary Neville at the side of the area and his low ball across the six-yard box finds Paul Scholes at the back post. Scholes makes no mistake as he completes a 17-minute hat-trick that seals the three points early in the second half.

3 May 2003

Ruud van Nistelrooy scores his 43rd goal of the campaign to put United 4-1 up and seal three vital points as the Reds move to within touching distance of the title. David Beckham's superb crossfield pass from the right lands straight at the feet of the Dutch striker who controls it in an instant before sweeping home a low shot that beats the keeper on his near post. The game is played in front of a Premier League record crowd of 67,721. There are no further goals and when Arsenal lose 3-2 at home to Leeds United the next day, United are confirmed as champions without kicking a ball with the Gunners no longer able to catch them at the top of the table.

27 January 2010

Paul Scholes finally puts United 1-0 up against Manchester City in the League Cup semi-final second leg at Old Trafford. The Reds had trailed 2-1 from the first leg at the Etihad and though City hold out for 52 minutes, the ball falls to Scholes on the edge of the box after Nani's run is blocked and the England midfielder's first-time daisy-cutter of a shot arrows into the bottom-left corner to level the aggregate scores.

7 August 2011

After going 2-0 down to Manchester City in a hotly contested FA Community Shield derby at Wembley, the Reds begin an astonishing comeback. Ashley Young's free kick on the left, midway inside the City half, floats into the box and Chris Smalling gets in behind the defence to guide a volley past Joe Hart from four yards out to halve the deficit.

53

29 May 1968

Playing in the European Cup Final for the first time, United take on Benfica at Wembley Stadium. After a tentative first half, the Reds – playing in an all-navy blue strip – finally take the lead as the ball falls to David Sadler on the left flank and his cross into the box sees Bobby Charlton rise to glance a superb header past Benfica keeper José Henrique and just inside the right-hand post to make it 1-0.

4 March 1995

Three Ipswich Town defenders surround Mark Hughes on the edge of the box but they can't wrestle the Welsh striker off the ball and he instead feeds a pass to the right where Denis Irwin crosses into the middle and Andy Cole scruffily heads home from close range to complete his hat-trick and put the Reds 4-0 up.

25 November 1998

United go 2-1 up against Barcelona at the Camp Nou with a goal that is thanks to the understanding between Andy Cole and Dwight Yorke. The pair exchange several passes outside the Barca box as they dissect the Catalans' defence and Cole finishes with a clever low shot to the left after feigning to go right.

22 May 1999

Premier League champions United go 2-0 up against Newcastle in the 1999 FA Cup Final and it is the same combination that created the opening goal. In the first half, Paul Scholes had set up Teddy Sheringham to score and the roles are reversed as Sheringham sets up Scholes to double the Reds' lead. United press forward with Ryan Giggs before the ball is partially cleared by the Magpies. Ole Gunnar Solskjaer then drives towards the box, finding Sheringham, who instantly tees up Scholes to drive a low shot home from the edge of the box to keep Sir Alex Ferguson's men on course for an unprecedented treble.

23 November 2002

Ruud van Nistelrooy completes his hat-trick with all of his goals scored inside the six-yard box. Newcastle had just reduced the Reds' lead to 3-2 with a stunning Alan Shearer free kick but within a minute, United restore their two-goal advantage. Mikael Silvestre's clever pass down the left flank finds Diego Forlan and the Uruguayan looks to have delayed his cross too long before drawing two defenders and the keeper in and then managing to find van Nistelrooy with a smart cross – and the Dutchman converts with a cushioned header to make it 4-2.

19 May 2013

United stem West Brom's fightback to go 4-2 up at The Hawthorns in an entertaining final-day clash with West

Brom. It's a landmark goal, too, as Antonio Valencia cuts a ball back into the box from the right and Robin van Persie sweeps a shot home from eight yards and claims his 30th of his debut season for the Reds.

7 April 2017

Rarely has a party been spoiled in quite the manner United would delay Manchester City's title confirmation. Needing a win to give Pep Guardiola his first Premier League title, City score twice in the first half to go into the break at the Etihad 2-0 up. It was the scenario no United fan wanted, but what followed was an extraordinary 16-minute spell by the Reds that turned the game on its head. They get back to 2-1 as Alexis Sanchez weaves space for himself on the right flank before pinging a ball into the middle that is chested superbly by Ander Herrera into the path of Paul Pogba, who coolly slots home past Ederson.

54

22 December 2001

Paul Scholes is again the creator – his second assist of the game – as United go 4-0 up against Southampton at Old Trafford. Scholes manages to get a toe to the ball and send Ruud van Nistelrooy clear. The Dutchman enters the box slightly to the left, from where he unleashes a low, left-footed shot across keeper Paul Jones and into the bottom-right corner.

55

21 May 1977

United re-take the lead against Liverpool in the 1977 FA Cup Final with a goal that has more than a slice of good fortune about it. With Liverpool levelling just two minutes before, the Reds are straight back on the attack and as Jimmy Greenhoff wrestles for possession in the Liverpool box, Lou Macari is first to the loose ball and his shot at goal strikes the chest of Greenhoff on its way into the back of the net to give United a 2-1 lead that won't be relinquished.

21 May 1983

A surging run from right-back Mike Duxbury results in United equalising against Brighton & Hove Albion in the 1983 FA Cup Final. Duxbury plays a smart one-two with Alan Davies before playing an accidental one-two with Brighton's Jimmy Case and getting to the right of the Seagulls' box and crossing towards the near post, where Norman Whiteside gets a glancing header that cuts out the keeper and Frank Stapleton slides the ball home at the far post to make it 1-1 at Wembley.

4 March 1995

Two goals in the space of three minutes effectively end the contest against Ipswich Town as United go

5-0 up at Old Trafford. Mark Hughes had been heavily involved on three of the four goals already scored but it is the Welshman who deservedly scores number five himself. Ryan Giggs torments the Ipswich defenders as he runs at them with pace on the left and his cross into the centre is met by Hughes at the back post where he sends a rocket half-volley in off the underside of the crossbar from a tight angle to give the keeper no chance.

21 October 1998

A clinical finish by skipper Roy Keane restores United's three-goal Champions League advantage against Brondby. A smart passing move on the right of the box ends with Dwight Yorke finding the run of Keane, who strikes a low shot that cannons into the net off the foot of the left post to make it 4-1.

23 November 2002

United go 5-2 up with a second goal in the space of three minutes against Newcastle. Mikael Silvestre is heavily involved for the fourth time in the game with a superb 40-yard pass putting Ole Gunnar Solskjaer clear. The Norwegian chests the ball down and then fires a low shot into the bottom-left corner to all-but seal three points for the rampant Reds.

26 February 2006

United double their lead over Wigan Athletic in the League Cup Final at the Millennium Stadium. Ryan

Giggs superbly weaves his way out of trouble on the halfway line before sending a lofted pass out to Cristiano Ronaldo on the right flank. Ronaldo waits before playing a simple pass to the overlapping Gary Neville, who sends a low square cross into the six-yard box where Louis Saha sees his initial shot blocked by keeper John Filan, but only against Saha and back over Filan and into the net to make it 2-0. It is Saha's sixth of the season in the League Cup.

7 April 2017

A second goal in the space of two minutes stuns the Etihad as United fight back to make it 2-2 against Manchester City. The Blues, needing a victory to seal Pep Guardiola's first Premier League title, had gone in two goals up at the break but Pep's old adversary José Mourinho will have the final say on this occasion. Alexis Sanchez is given too much time as he moves into the City half and the Chilean spots Paul Pogba's surging run, picking him out with a delightful chip, and the French midfielder expertly nods the ball past Ederson from close range to level the scores to turn this thrilling Manchester derby on its head.

26 September 2020

Marcus Rashford's superb individual goal puts United 2-1 up against Brighton & Hove Albion at the Amex Stadium. Rashford collects a pass on the left flank before driving into the Seagulls' box. He cuts inside of one challenge, then another before checking back the other way and seating a defender on his backside before rifling a powerful shot into the top-right corner of the net, via one of the grounded defenders. Sublime from the striker.

56

29 August 1908

George Wall gets the goal his all-round performance merits as he puts United 3-0 up in the FA Charity Shield replay at Stamford Bridge. Sandy Turnbull's first-half brace had put the Reds in command and Jack Picken is the creator of the third, picking out Wall who finishes from close range.

11 December 2011

Michael Carrick doubles United's lead at Queens Park Rangers. The Reds had led through Wayne Rooney's first-minute header and Carrick gives his side breathing space when he collects a poor pass from former City midfielder Joey Barton before shrugging off Alejandro Faurlin's challenge and then drilling a crisp shot past the keeper from the edge of the box.

57

25 May 1963

United double the lead in the FA Cup Final as Matt Busby looks to oversee the Reds' third triumph in the competition as well as win it for the second time as manager. The goal comes as Bobby Charlton's low shot is parried across the six-yard box by Leicester City keeper Gordon Banks and David Herd is on hand to roll the ball into the empty net to make it 2-0.

1 November 2008

United score from a corner for the second time to go 4-1 up against a Hull City side who had been previously unbeaten away from home in the Premier League that season. This time, Wayne Rooney's corner is glanced on at the near post by Rio Ferdinand and Nemanja Vidic, just behind his central defensive partner, is the beneficiary as he prods the ball past the keeper from a couple of yards out. The Reds will go on to win the game, but the Tigers pull a couple of goals back to leave Old Trafford with a more respectable 4-3 defeat.

58

3 August 1997

Ronny Johnsen levels the scores in the FA Charity Shield clash with Chelsea at Wembley. United had fallen behind just six minutes earlier when Mark Hughes scored against his former employers, but the Reds get back on level terms when Ryan Giggs's corner is headed downwards and into the bottom-left corner by Johnsen.

4 December 1999

Ole Gunnar Solskjaer grabs his fourth goal of the game – and United's fifth – as the Reds go 5-1 up against Everton with not even an hour played. The unfortunate Richard Dunne – who had given away the penalty that allowed the Reds to equalise in the first half – gives the ball away to Ryan Giggs, who sees his shot deflect kindly into the Norwegian striker's path and he makes no mistake from six yards with a low finish from close range. All Solskjaer's goals have come in an incredible 29-minute burst as he proves there are other options than Andy Cole and Dwight Yorke – should Alex Ferguson need them.

29 September 2001

Nails are bitten just a little quicker by the Tottenham fans as United pull another goal back at White Hart

Lane. It's a fairly simple set-piece that does it as David Beckham's outswinging corner is met firmly by the head of Laurent Blanc to make it 3-2 in Spurs' favour.

12 April 2003

United complete the scoring for the afternoon, declaring on six as punch-drunk Newcastle reel at St James' Park. With what will be the Reds' sixth goal in 26 devastating minutes, the Magpies are the architects of their own demise when a hashed clearance sees Titus Bramble pull Diego Forlan down in the box and Ruud van Nistelrooy strokes home the resulting spot-kick to make it 6-1. The win puts United three points clear of Arsenal in a knife-edge title race with only five games remaining – and a trip to face the Gunners next on the schedule just four days later.

17 April 2005

A shocking pass from former United favourite Nicky Butt ends with the Reds all-but sealing a place in the FA Cup Final. Newcastle midfielder Butt's attempt to find a team-mate just inside the United half falls way short and United break quickly. When Wayne Rooney is denied on the edge of the Magpies' box, Paul Scholes plays a short pass to his right and Ruud van Nistelrooy calmly slots a low shot past Shay Given to make it 3-0 at the Millennium Stadium.

7 August 2011

United's second goal in six minutes makes it 2-2 in a thrilling FA Community Shield clash against neighbours

Manchester City at Wembley. A determined United wipe out City's two-goal half-time lead with a superbly worked second as Nani plays a short pass to Wayne Rooney on the edge of the box and his back-flick to Tom Cleverley is then worked on to Nani, who continues his run before collecting the ball and firing an angled shot into the roof of the net.

59

17 May 1990

Few footballers get to say they scored the winning goal in the FA Cup Final, but United's Lee Martin joins a select club when he scores the only goal of the replay with Crystal Palace. The first game had ended 3-3 five days earlier, but this will be the Reds' night as Danny Wallace plays a short pass in from the right flank to Neil Webb who spots left-back Martin's burst towards the box, chips a lofted pass into his path and Martin chests the ball down before firing an unstoppable shot into the roof of the net from the corner of the six-yard box to give the Reds a seventh FA Cup triumph and a fourth in 13 years.

4 March 1995

With not quite an hour gone, United go 6-0 up against Ipswich Town at Old Trafford. Brian McClair sends Ryan Giggs through and the winger sees his shot well saved by keeper Craig Forrest, but the ball loops up and Mark Hughes leaps to nod into the empty net for his second of the afternoon – his fifth involvement in a goal of the game.

22 August 1999

Roy Keane equalises for United at Arsenal. Paul Scholes wins possession from Patrick Vieira and plays it to

Keane, who spots Andy Cole on the edge of the box, plays a low ball into his feet and then runs into the box for the return pass before calmly knocking it past the keeper to make it 1-1 in a tense Premier League clash.

30 March 2002

United go 4-1 up just before the hour with a well-worked goal at Elland Road. David Beckham races down the right flank unchallenged and has the time to pick out Ryan Giggs on the edge of the six-yard box and despite the presence of a couple of Leeds defenders, the Welsh winger confidently side-foots home to put the game beyond the hosts – though Leeds will pull a couple of goals back in a frantic finish that ends in a 4-3 win for the Reds.

26 February 2006

Wigan Athletic are masters of their own downfall when a poor clearance leads to United going 3-0 up in the 2006 League Cup Final. As the Latics defence go into an 'anywhere will do' mood, Stephane Henchoz hits the ball straight to Louis Saha, who collects and plays a quick pass out to Cristiano Ronaldo on the right of the Wigan box. Ronaldo takes a touch before drilling a low, angled shot into the bottom-left corner to put the Reds out of sight at the Millennium Stadium.

24 April 2007

An outrageous pass from Paul Scholes brings United level against AC Milan at Old Trafford. Though the Reds had made an ideal start with Cristiano Ronaldo's early goal, two brilliant efforts from Kaka had put the Italian giants firmly in control of the Champions League semi-final first leg at Old Trafford. But the Reds equalise just before the hour as Scholes lifts a pass over several defenders with the outside of his boot and Wayne Rooney does the rest, getting just enough on the ball to beat the keeper and make it 2-2 on the night.

11 August 2013

Robin van Persie puts United 2-0 up against Wigan Athletic in the FA Community Shield at Wembley as the Reds – and the prolific Dutch striker – get off to the perfect start to life under David Moyes. As United attack looking for a second against the Championship side, Danny Welbeck finds van Persie just inside the Latics' box. He works himself a yard of space before unleashing a left-footed drive that James Perch wafts a leg at and takes it away from keeper Scott Carson and into the bottom-right corner to complete the scoring.

60

27 April 1908

Appearing in the inaugural FA Charity Shield match – which was between the winners of the Football League and the winners of the Southern League at that time – Billy Meredith equalises for United. Jimmy Bannister finds Meredith on the wing, tormenting QPR's left-back throughout, and as he nears the box the Welsh superstar shoots from 20 yards past the keeper to make it 1-1 in a game held at Chelsea's Stamford Bridge.

20 August 1983

United take a decisive 2-0 lead over Liverpool in the FA Charity Shield clash at Wembley. It's no more than the Reds deserve based on chances and while the opening goal had been a work of art, the second is anything but as Jesper Olsen's corner is flicked on at the near post by Gordon McQueen, Frank Stapleton stoops to head towards goal and Sammy Lee clears off the line but Bryan Robson is on hand to bundle the ball home for his second of the game.

3 May 1993

United take the lead on the hour against Blackburn Rovers with a Paul Ince goal. Eric Cantona tries to play a through ball on the edge of the box but a Rovers player toes it back to him. Given a second chance, he then plays a ball into the box and Ince slides in to force the ball home and make it 2-1.

14 May 1994

After an hour of play, United finally break the deadlock in the 1994 FA Cup Final after Denis Irwin is scythed down in the box by Chelsea defender Eddie Newton, giving referee David Elleray an easy decision to point to the spot. Eric Cantona steps up to take the penalty, sending keeper Dmitri Kharine the wrong way and make it 1-0 at Wembley.

21 October 1998

United's Danish romp continues. Brondby have no answers to stop the rampant Reds and Dwight Yorke finally gets his name on the scoresheet as he heads Phil Neville's cross from the left into the bottom-right corner to make it 5-1 on the night – with only an hour played.

10 April 2007

Michael Carrick scores his second stunning goal of the evening to put United 6-1 up against Roma. A Cristiano Ronaldo cross from the right is too deep and ends up with Gabriel Heinze on the left of the box. The Argentine spots Carrick in space 20 yards out, passes to him and with the United fans urging him to shoot, he does just that, hitting a powerful shot that arrows into the top-right corner to put the Reds 7-3 up on aggregate and en route to the Champions League semi-finals.

61

26 February 2006

A third goal in six minutes ends the League Cup Final as a contest as Wigan Athletic capitulate. A Ryan Giggs free kick finds its way to the head of Rio Ferdinand, who nods down to Wayne Rooney in the six-yard box and he immediately swivels and drives a shot into the back of the net from a couple of yards out to seal a 4-0 victory over the Latics at the Millennium Stadium in what is United's second League Cup triumph.

13 May 2008

Just four minutes after climbing off the bench, Carlos Tevez levels for United away to Wigan Athletic – and what a goal it is. Michael Carrick fires a low shot towards goal and Tevez, back to goal, diverts the ball into the bottom-right corner with a brilliant back flick that gives the keeper no chance and makes the score 1-1.

5 May 2009

Cristiano Ronaldo wraps up victory for United, who make it to a second Champions League Final in succession. With their side 2-0 down at the Emirates and 3-0 behind on aggregate, any lingering hopes the Arsenal fans were clinging on to is ended by a counter attack that sees Ji-Sung Park feed Wayne Rooney to his left and Rooney's clever pass through the legs of a defender is perfect for Ronaldo to run on to and sweep a low drive home from ten yards to make it 3-0.

62

7 February 1970

The George Best show continues as he grabs his fourth goal of the game away to Northampton Town. Brian Kidd's first cross from the left is cleared back to him, and he sends another fine ball towards the six-yard box where Best steals in to glance a superb diving header into the bottom-right corner for his fourth of the afternoon at the County Ground.

26 May 1983

Game, set and match as the Reds go 4-0 up in the FA Cup Final against Brighton. Man of the match Bryan Robson, already with two goals to his name, wrestles for the ball with defender Gary Stevens and as Robson pulls up appealing for a foul, the linesman flags for a penalty and Arnold Muhren steps up to stroke the ball into the bottom-right corner to complete the Wembley rout over the Seagulls.

12 May 1990

Mark Hughes thumps home an angled shot to put United 2-1 up against Crystal Palace in the FA Cup Final. Palace had blocked a couple of attempts to cross the ball in but as an attempted clearance is blocked by Neil Webb, the ball deflects into the path of Hughes, who emphatically beats keeper Nigel Martyn with a powerful rising shot into the right of the net.

21 October 1998

United go 6-1 up away to Brondby. The Danes must have been fearing a cricket score on their own soil as Ole Gunnar Solskjaer drills a precise low shot into the bottom-right corner from 18 yards after a smart lay-off by Dwight Yorke. The Reds declare at six and the hosts will pull one back, though it is scant consolation after conceding six in their own stadium.

4 November 1998

Paul Scholes completes the scoring against Brondby at Old Trafford with a fine individual goal, cutting in from the right, drifting past a couple of defenders before tucking a low left-footed shot into the bottom-right corner to make it 5-0.

27 November 2010

Dimitar Berbatov makes it 6-0 against Sam Allardyce's Blackburn Rovers with little more than an hour played at Old Trafford. As with most of the goals in this game, it is all way too easy as Rafael bursts into the box from the right before teeing up Ji-Sung Park, who sees his low shot from close range blocked by Samba, and Berbatov is on hand to drill home from a few yards out for his fourth of the evening.

21 April 2018

Ander Herrera scores the goal that sends United to the FA Cup Final. The Reds come from behind to beat Tottenham Hotspur 2-1 when Alexis Sanchez collects the ball on the left of the Londoners' box and attempts to find Romelu Lukaku but the Belgian can only divert it inadvertently to Jesse Lingard, who immediately lays it off for Herrera to strike a low shot into the middle of the goal and past an unsighted Michel Vorm.

63

18 December 1999

Having led 3-0 after 20 minutes, United are clinging to the advantage away to West Ham, who have reduced the deficit to just one thanks to a couple of Paolo Di Canio goals. But the Reds get vital breathing space again when Ryan Giggs uses his considerable pace to leave the Hammers' defence for dead and his cross is turned home by Dwight Yorke for what will be the final goal in a 4-2 win at Upton Park.

1 April 2000

Nicky Butt is denied a rare goal as he is tripped by West Ham's John Moncur, resulting in a penalty. David Beckham sends a lofted ball into Butt's path and the combative midfielder gets to it before keeper Craig Forrest, delicately lifting it over him and as he's about to finish and score, Moncur taps his ankle and brings him down. With Denis Irwin missing a penalty in the first half, Paul Scholes steps up to hammer a rising shot into the centre of the net, completing his hat-trick in the process and putting the Reds 5-1 up.

16 April 2003

Moments after going 2-1 down to Arsenal at Highbury, United are back on level terms in a game neither side can afford to lose. The Reds went into the match three points clear at the top but having played one game more as well as having an inferior goal difference. To respond immediately stemmed the tide that seemed to be edging the title towards north London, so when Paul Scholes feeds Ole Gunnar Solskjaer on the right of the Arsenal box, he lofts a cross towards the back post where Ryan Giggs ghosts in to head the ball down and past keeper Stuart Taylor to make it 2-2. It will be a pivotal point in a thrilling Premier League title race.

19 May 2013

It looks like game, set and match for United as Javier Hernandez puts the Reds 5-2 up against West Brom. Ryan Giggs threads an excellent low cross into the six-yard box from the left and the Mexican is on hand to tap home from close in for his 50th goal in United colours. Incredibly, the hosts will fight back to draw 5-5 and ensure Sir Alex Ferguson's final match in charge doesn't end in victory.

64

21 April 1993

A stunning Mark Hughes volley finally breaks down Crystal Palace's stubborn resistance at Selhurst Park. Inevitably, Eric Cantona is involved as he takes the ball down the left flank before sending a perfectly weighted chip towards the right corner of the six-yard box where Hughes hits a thumping first-time shot past the keeper to put the Reds 1-0 up.

16 September 1998

Having seen a 2-0 first-half lead wiped out in 15 second-half minutes by Barcelona, United quickly regain the advantage. From a free kick 30 yards out and slightly left of centre, David Beckham strikes a sweet, curling shot over the wall and into the top-left corner for a stunning goal that puts the Reds 3-2 up on an absorbing Champions League night at Old Trafford.

20 August 2006

Wayne Rooney scores his second and the Reds' fifth against Fulham after a fine move down the right flank. Cristiano Ronaldo puts Wes Brown clear and the defender plays a fine cross into the box where the waiting Rooney side-foots a low shot into the bottom-left corner to make it 5-1 on a dream opening day for the Reds.

28 August 2011

Wayne Rooney curls a sumptuous free kick home to put United 4-1 up against Arsenal. It's a set-piece masterclass from Rooney, who had already scored a beauty in the first half before lifting the ball over the Gunners' wall and into the far left of the net with a deftly swerving shot.

George Best lets fly past the challenge of Manuel Sanchis to score the only goal of the European Cup semi-final, first-leg match at Old Trafford against Real Madrid. 24 April 1968

George Best sends a diving header past Northampton Town keeper Kim Book to complete a double hat-trick in an FA Cup tie at the County Ground. United will win 8-2. 9 February 1970

Bobby Charlton leaps into the air in celebration after scoring the first goal of the European Cup Final against Benfica. 29 May 1968

Bobby Charlton glances a superb header past Benfica goalkeeper Jose Henrique to score the opening goal of the 1968 European Cup Final at Wembley. 29 May 1968

Stuart Pearson (left) and Steve Coppell congratulate Jimmy Greenhoff (on ground) after scoring the first goal against Leeds United during the FA Cup semi-final game, 1977

Denis Law challenges Leicester City keeper Gordon Banks in the 1963 FA Cup Final. 25 May 1963

Denis Law sends Benfica goalkeeper Costa Pereira the wrong way to put United into a 2-1 lead in the European Cup quarter-final, first leg at Old Trafford. 2 February 1966

United manager Tommy Docherty celebrates with the lid of the FA Cup after his team's 2-1 victory over Liverpool at Wembley. 21 May 1977

A furious Kevin Moran is shown the red card in the FA Cup Final against Everton at Wembley. Ten-man United will go on to win the game 1-0. 18 May 1985

Danny Wallace celebrates his part in Bryan Robson's equalising goal against Crystal Palace in the 1990 FA Cup final at Wembley. 12 May 1990

Ryan Giggs's spectacular extra-time winner against Arsenal at Villa Park. 14 April 1999

United's Teddy Sheringham celebrates after equalising against Bayern Munich in the UEFA Champions League Final. 26 May 1999

Ole Gunnar Solskjaer scores a dramatic added-time winner against Bayern Munich to clinch the 1999 Champions League Final and an historic treble for the Reds. 26 May 1999

Patrice Evra, Nemanja Vidic and John O'Shea celebrate the 2008 Champions League win over Chelsea in Moscow. 21 May 2008

Scott McTominay celebrates United's second goal against Manchester City in the final game before lockdown in March 2020. It completes a 2-0 win for the Reds.

65

4 March 1995

The irrepressible Mark Hughes is again at the heart of the move that sees United go 7-0 up against Ipswich Town. Andy Cole finds Hughes 35 yards from goal in the middle of the Ipswich half and his first-time ball into the path of Brian McClair sees the Scot with just the keeper to beat, but as his low shot is saved, Cole – who had followed the move he began – is first to the loose ball to turn home his fourth of the game with a clinical finish from eight yards out.

11 May 1996

Eric Cantona scores the goal that settles the FA Cup Final against Liverpool – and what a strike. United win a corner on the right and David Beckham takes it, sending the ball into the Liverpool box where keeper David James jumps up to punch clear but it only goes as far as the edge of the box, where Cantona slightly adjusts his stance before sending a powerful volley through a sea of bodies and into the back of the net. A superb strike and enough to give the Reds a 1-0 win at Wembley as well as completing a second league and cup double in the space of three years.

30 August 1999

Andy Cole completes his hat-trick against former club Newcastle United at Old Trafford. Ryan Giggs plays a defence-splitting pass from the left and Cole sneaks in behind the last defender to collect and then plant a low shot past Tommy Wright to put United 3-1 up against the managerless visitors.

1 December 2002

What seems like the end of a United attack results in the Reds taking a 1-0 lead against Liverpool at Anfield. A long ball from keeper Fabien Barthez is nodded on but only as far as defender Jamie Carragher, who heads it back to his own keeper Jerzy Dudek – but as the Pole goes down to gather the simplest of balls, it somehow squirms under his body and Diego Forlan is first to tap the ball into the empty net.

22 May 2004

United go 2-0 up in the 2004 FA Cup Final at Cardiff's Millennium Stadium and though it is Ruud van Nistelrooy who scores, Ryan Giggs is the creator. Giggs dances in from the left, going past a defender before cutting between two more as he moves towards the corner of the six-yard box and is brought down by a crude tackle from David Livermore. Referee Jeff Winter awards a penalty and van Nistelrooy thumps the spot-kick high into the top-left corner to put the Reds 2-0 up against the second-tier side.

66

17 April 1971

Denis Law completes his hat-trick as United make it two goals in two minutes to go 5-2 up against Crystal Palace at Selhurst Park. United had been 2-0 down after 24 minutes but a treble from Law and a brace from George Best means the rampant Reds all-but seal victory as Paddy Crerand intercepts a poor ball on the right of the Palace box before sending a low cross into the box that Law sweeps home into the bottom-left corner.

14 May 1994

Chelsea concede a second penalty in the space of six minutes in the FA Cup Final. Andrei Kanchelskis looks to have the legs on Frank Sinclair as he enters the box but the centre-half barges him to the floor and the referee awards a spot-kick. In today's world of VAR, the decision may well have been overruled as a shoulder charge – and one that starts outside the box – but Eric Cantona cares little, tucking the ball into the bottom-right corner and sending Dmitri Kharine the wrong way to make it 2-0 to the Reds at Wembley.

4 January 1998

A defence-splitting pass from Ryan Giggs sets up United's fourth goal of the FA Cup third round tie against Chelsea. Giggs receives the ball on the halfway line before threading it between two Chelsea defenders for Andy Cole to race on to and the striker beats Ed de Goey with a low shot across goal into the bottom-right corner, to make it 4-0 and seemingly seal victory.

25 November 1998

United and Barcelona continue to slug it out in an enthralling clash at the Camp Nou. The Reds had been 1-0 down, then went 2-1 up and been pegged back to 2-2 when David Beckham's perfect cross from the right is headed past the keeper to make it 3-2. Though the game will end just as the first Champions League group stage clash had done in a 3-3 draw, it is a fantastic result for United in what is very much a group of death. It also means that the Reds had scored 19 goals in five group stage matches – with not one coming after the 66th minute.

1 April 2000

David Beckham scores a stunning free kick in front of the Stretford End as United take a 6-1 lead over West Ham at Old Trafford. When Paul Scholes is fouled 25 yards out, Scholes and Beckham stand over the ball – but it is Beckham who steps up, curling a superb shot into the top-left corner and giving the Hammers keeper no chance, via the underside of the crossbar. Postage-stamp stuff.

20 December 2020

Daniel James scores to make it 5-1 against Leeds United as the Old Trafford rout continues. Scott McTominay – scorer of the first two goals – turns provider as he cuts in from the left, just inside the Leeds half before fizzing a low pass towards the edge of the box where James's first touch takes him away from two defenders and he finishes with a left-footed shot that goes through the keeper's legs.

67

15 May 1991

United take the lead in the 1991 European Cup Winners' Cup Final against Barcelona. The match, held in Rotterdam, had been on a knife-edge until the Reds win a central free kick 35 yards from goal. Bryan Robson takes the set-piece, floating a curling free kick into the box where Steve Bruce meets it and heads towards goal. With the Barca keeper Carles Busquets stranded off his line the ball is clearly on its way in before Mark Hughes snatches it away from Bruce by getting the final touch almost on the goal line – nobody is too bothered though as the Reds go 1-0 up.

18 November 1991

United, playing in the European Super Cup at Old Trafford in front of 22,110 fans, score the only goal of what is later described as 'one of the most boring European finals of all time'. It was clearly a competition few had interest in judging by the thousands of empty seats at Old Trafford. Brian McClair scores the only goal of the game midway through the second half when Neil Webb goes past Dejan Savićević on the edge of the box, and sees his shot deflected on to the post by keeper Zvonko Milojevic with McClair on hand to jab home the rebound and secure a 1-0 win on a largely forgettable evening for all concerned.

6 February 1999

A strange but welcome fourth for the Reds against Nottingham Forest at the City Ground. Jesper Blomqvist attacks the left of the Forest box and takes on the full-back before hitting a low cross in that is deflected on to the foot of the post by a Forest defender and straight to Dwight Yorke, who taps into the net from a couple of yards for one of the easiest goals he will ever score.

1 December 2002

Diego Forlan scores his second goal in two minutes to silence Anfield. If his first goal had been a gift after a mistake by keeper Jerzy Dudek, his second is anything but as Paul Scholes finds Ryan Giggs, who skips through a couple of challenges as he is surrounded by Liverpool players on the edge of the box. That allows him to play in Forlan on the right and the Uruguayan takes a touch before firing a powerful rising drive that beats Dudek on his near post and puts United 2-0 up and on the way to three points.

28 August 2011

United continue the rout of Arsène Wenger's Arsenal at Old Trafford. Chris Smalling bursts into the Gunners' half before finding Wayne Rooney, who spots Nani in space and the Portuguese forward does the rest, impudently dinking the ball over Wojciech Szczęsny to put the Reds 5-1 up.

3 November 2012

United double their lead over Arsenal at Old Trafford with a well-worked goal. Wayne Rooney takes a short corner to Ashley Young, who plays the ball back to Rooney on the left of the Gunners' box. The striker's cross into the six-yard box finds Patrice Evra, who heads home from close range to make it 2-0.

12 April 2015

United go 3-1 up in the Manchester derby at Old Trafford. Wayne Rooney receives the ball from the left flank, midway inside the City half, and he plays an immediate pass into the path of Juan Mata, who keeps his cool as he closes in on goal before sliding a low shot past Joe Hart to put clear daylight between the rivals.

4 May 2017

A wonderful free kick from Marcus Rashford gives United a crucial 1-0 lead away to Celta Vigo in the Europa League semi-final first leg. The Reds had squandered several good chances when an infringement on the right edge of the La Liga side's box is penalised. Rashford takes it, whipping an angled shot over the wall that curls away into the right of the goal to give the keeper no chance – a fantastic strike.

25 September 2018

Sergio Romero, on a rare appearance for United, is shown a straight red card in the League Cup tie with Derby County at Old Trafford. The Argentine reserve keeper races out to stop the Rams' Harry Wilson, who tries to knock the ball past him. Romero instinctively stops it with his arm and is dismissed by the referee for denying a clear goalscoring opportunity. Though the score is 1-1 at the time, United will eventually lose on penalties to Frank Lampard's Championship side.

68

13 February 2005

In a scrappy Manchester derby, United take the lead at the Etihad. The Reds, needing to win to at least have some hope of catching runaway leaders Chelsea, edge in front against City when Gary Neville's low ball in from the right flank is turned home by Wayne Rooney at the near post to make it 1-0.

30 November 2008

A bizarre Manchester derby moment as Wayne Rooney's cross is almost caught by Cristiano Ronaldo on the near post, leading to a second booking and a red card for the Portuguese forward. It seems Ronaldo is maybe caught in two minds, but it proves one of the strangest dismissals in the history of this fixture, even though the ten-man Reds hold out to win 1-0 at the Etihad.

25 September 2019

Mason Greenwood finally breaks down a stubborn Rochdale defence to put United 1-0 up in the League Cup third round at Old Trafford. Greenwood cuts past one challenge inside the box and finishes with a smart, low right-foot drive into the bottom-right corner following Jesse Lingard's pass. The visitors will level shortly afterwards and force a tense penalty shoot-out.

69

14 May 1994

Yet another blunder by the Chelsea defence sees Mark Hughes profit as the Reds go 3-0 up in the 1994 FA Cup Final. Having conceded two penalties in the space of six minutes, Glenn Hoddle's men again hit self-destruct as Frank Sinclair mis-controls the ball into Hughes's path and the Welsh striker buries a low shot into the bottom-left corner from 12 yards to complete a crazy nine-minute spell in which United had blown away the west London side.

27 April 2003

United finally break Tottenham's resistance at White Hart Lane. In a game that could see the Reds go five points clear at the top of the table with only three matches remaining, Kasey Keller in the Spurs goal manages to keep his side level with a series of fine saves before he is finally beaten. David Beckham fires a 40-yard pass towards the edge of the box where Paul Scholes cleverly heads backwards out to Ryan Giggs. Giggs controls the ball before sending a tempting cross into the six-yard box for Scholes to head home from a couple of yards out and put United 1-0 up.

7 April 2017

In an uncanny comeback that almost exactly replicated the 2011 FA Community Shield against Manchester City, United come from two goals down to win 3-2 and deny the Blues a Premier League title in the process. In 2011, United had been 2-0 down at Wembley but scored twice before the hour to level. The same thing happens in this clash – at the Etihad – after Paul Pogba bagged a brace but the winner comes earlier on this occasion as Alexis Sanchez floats a free kick into the six-yard box for Chris Smalling to ghost in and volley home from close range – almost an identical goal to his volley at Wembley six years earlier.

2 February 2021

Some 30 minutes had passed since United's fourth goal as Southampton battled to stem the tide, but the fifth goal of the night once again sees the ten-man Saints start to capitulate. Bruno Fernandes chips the ball to the edge of the six-yard box for Anthony Martial who chests the pass down, takes one touch and then rockets an angled shot into the roof of the net to make it 5-0.

70

24 April 1948

Jack Rowley scores his second goal of the game as United equalise for the second time in the FA Cup Final at Wembley. Blackpool had twice led, but the Reds pull level when Rowley nods home following a Johnny Morris free kick on the right of the box.

6 February 1957

Tommy Taylor puts United level on aggregate and ahead on away goals in a dramatic European Cup second-round tie at Maine Road. With Old Trafford not ready to host midweek ties yet, City lend their home ground – and floodlights (!) as the Reds fight back against Athletic Bilbao, who won a dramatic first leg 5-3. Taylor's strike puts United 2-0 up on the night to make it 5-5 on aggregate and the Reds will score again five minutes from the end to progress to the next round.

27 November 2010

It's goal number five for Dimitar Berbatov as he moves to within one of a double hat-trick against Blackburn Rovers. It is clearly the Bulgarian's day as he moves into the box and tries to play a cross to the unmarked Wayne Rooney, only to see the blocked cross land at his feet. He drills home a low shot to make it 7-0 with 20 minutes still to play. The Reds declare at seven and the visitors even pull one back with their first shot on target as the game eventually ends 7-1.

28 August 2011

Old Trafford rises again as United go 6-1 up against Arsenal. The Gunners' defending is once more poor as the Reds work an opportunity after Ashley Young plays a short pass back to Ji-Sung Park on the edge of the box and the South Korean does the rest, sending a low, angled shot past the unsighted Wojciech Szczęsny and into the bottom-right corner.

20 December 2020

United get goal number six from the penalty spot against Leeds. Marcus Rashford interchanges with Anthony Martial inside the box and the French forward is tripped as he tries to work a yard of space. Bruno Fernandes steps up to send the keeper the wrong way and put the Reds 6-1 up in a game that will end 6-2 at Old Trafford.

7 January 2020

Marcus Rashford gives United a glimmer of hope in the League Cup semi-final first leg with Manchester City at Old Trafford. The Blues had been in red-hot form on the night and gone in 3-0 up at half-time, with the tie looking as good as over. But when Mason Greenwood intercepts a sloppy pass near the halfway line, he drives towards goal before playing a ball to his right and Rashford hits a low shot into the bottom-left corner.

71

1 October 1995

Eric Cantona announces his return after his lengthy ban for a kung-fu kick at Crystal Palace with the goal that levels the scores against Liverpool at Old Trafford. Cantona, who had already assisted Nicky Butt's opening goal, plays Ryan Giggs into the box where the Welsh winger is felled by Jamie Redknapp. The referee points to the spot and Cantona coolly slots the spot kick home, sending the keeper the wrong way before swinging around the net support as he celebrates making it 2-2.

30 August 1999

Andy Cole continues his one-man demolition of former employers Newcastle United as he bags his fourth of the afternoon. Perhaps the best of the lot, Cole receives a low pass to feet from Gary Neville and spins off his marker before firing an angled right-foot shot into the bottom-left corner and putting the Reds 4-1 up at Old Trafford.

14 February 2004

Ten-man United finally double their lead against Manchester City in a tempestuous FA Cup fifth round tie at Old Trafford. The Reds, who led 1-0 but saw Gary Neville sent off in the first half, make it 2-0 when City fail to clear the danger and when Cristiano Ronaldo receives the ball on the right, his low cross is turned in at the far post by Ruud van Nistelrooy, who then sets off in celebration waving his shirt around his head.

27 January 2010

Old Trafford goes wild as United go 2-0 up against City in the second leg of the League Cup semi-final. Nani clips a ball into the path of Darren Fletcher, who chests down before seeing a shot blocked. Fletcher has the nous to play a short pass to his right when the ball comes back to him and Michael Carrick drills a low shot into the bottom-left corner to put the Reds 3-2 up on aggregate.

2 February 2021

Scott McTominay gets in on the act as the Reds go 6-0 up against ten-man Southampton. His low pass to Mason Greenwood eventually sees a poor clearance to the edge of the box, where McTominay runs in to drill a daisy-cutter of a shot into the bottom-right corner with the keeper unsighted by a crowd of players in front of him.

72

7 February 1970

Sub Francis Burns wastes no time in claiming an assist as United go 6-0 up away to Northampton Town in the FA Cup. Burns sends a long pass into the path of George Best, who races to the edge of the Cobblers' box before slotting an angled low shot into the bottom-left corner for his fifth goal of the game.

21 May 1983

Ray Wilkins gives United the lead against Brighton & Hove Albion in the FA Cup Final. Wilkins moves towards the Seagulls' box before cutting inside and curling a beautiful shot over keeper Graham Moseley and into the top-left corner to make it 2-1 and send two thirds of Wembley into raptures – a superb strike by a very cultured footballer.

8 April 1990

Neil Webb puts United 2-1 up at Maine Road in the FA Cup semi-final derby with Oldham Athletic. The Reds attack down the right and a cross towards the left of the penalty area is nodded back across the six-yard box where former Nottingham Forest playmaker Webb just manages to get his head on it and direct it over the keeper and a defender to give his side the lead.

4 March 1995

Ipswich Town keeper Craig Forrest's nightmare at Old Trafford gets even worse as he rushes out to clear a long ball from the United half before Mark Hughes gets to it, but the ball brushes his hand 30 yards from goal and the referee awards a free kick. Paul Ince wrestles the ball out of Forrest's hands as the Tractor Boys' keeper casually trots back towards his goal. Ince then orchestrates a quick free kick that sees Hughes tap it right and Ince dinks the ball over the Ipswich players – and Forrest – and into the empty net to make it 8-0. The visitors complain but have only themselves to blame.

29 September 2001

United's incredible fightback continues as Ruud van Nistelrooy levels at White Hart Lane. Spurs had led 3-0 at the break, but when Mikael Silvestre gallops down the left and crosses in to the box, van Nistelrooy's head meets the ball and sends it past the keeper to make it 3-3 – the Reds' third headed goal of the game. But there is much more to come.

22 December 2001

The rout continues as United go 5-1 up against Southampton at Old Trafford. It's a well-worked fifth as well, with a nice combination of passes ending with Ruud van Nistelrooy finding Ryan Giggs, who immediately releases skipper Roy Keane with a delightful first-time half-volleyed pass. Keane runs between two Saints defenders before slotting a low shot past the keeper from 12 yards.

7 March 2007

Henrik Larsson scores the goal that seals victory over Lille and sends United into the Champions League quarter-finals. The on-loan Swedish striker – coming to the end of his ten-week temporary spell – heads home Cristiano Ronaldo's cross to make it 1-0 and complete a 2-0 aggregate victory over the French side.

73

1 April 2000

United go 7-1 up against West Ham – who had taken a 1-0 lead – to wrap up the scoring at Old Trafford. David Beckham – at the heart of this emphatic win – sends a ball into Teddy Sheringham on the edge of the box and his chested pass falls for Ole Gunnar Solskjaer who drills a low, angled shot past keeper Craig Forrest to bag the Reds' seventh of the afternoon. For Forrest, it's another Old Trafford nightmare having conceded nine with Ipswich Town a few years previously.

21 December 2008

Wayne Rooney scores the goal that settles the FIFA Club World Cup Final in Yokohama. Facing Ecuardorian side LDU Quito, the Reds had been reduced to ten men just after the start of the second half when Nemanja Vidic was sent off, but they hold firm and finally break through after a neat passing move sees Cristiano Ronaldo feed Rooney on the left of the Quito box. He sends a measured, right-footed shot low into the bottom corner from 15 yards.

14 May 2011

United are awarded a penalty away to Blackburn Rovers in a game they need only take a point from to win a record 19th top-flight title. Rovers, humiliated 7-1 at Old Trafford earlier in the campaign, are determined to spoil the party and had led through Brett Emerton's 20th-minute goal, but with time running out, the referee decides that Rovers keeper Paul Robinson had brought down Javier Hernandez and awards a spot-kick. Wayne Rooney keeps his cool to send Robinson the wrong way and make it 1-1 – and with no further goals at Ewood Park, it is enough to confirm that United are champions again.

12 April 2015

More poor defending by Manchester City is exploited by United, who go 4-1 up. Ashley Young curls in a free kick and Chris Smalling arrives in the six-yard box almost unchallenged to nod home past Joe Hart – taking advantage of a disjointed offside trap – in a game the Reds eventually win 4-2.

24 November 2019

With United facing a demoralising defeat away to Sheffield United, Brandon Williams starts a sizzling seven-minute spell that turns the game upside down. As a deep cross into the Blades' penalty area is only partially cleared, Williams hits a first-time shot from 12 yards that nestles in the bottom-right corner to bring United to within one goal of parity at Bramall Lane.

74

15 May 1991

Mark Hughes grabs his second goal in seven minutes to put United 2-0 up against Barcelona in the 1991 European Cup Winners' Cup Final. Bryan Robson is just inside the Barca half when he spots Hughes's run and dinks a beautiful pass into his path. The Welsh striker races clear, takes it around keeper Carles Busquets but looks to have pushed it too far wide – however, with one glance at the goal he fires a powerful low shot in from the right that gives the retreating defenders no chance as it fizzes past into the back of the net. Though the Catalans would pull a goal back, the Reds hold on to win 2-1 and claim the club's second major European trophy in the process.

4 January 1998

Ryan Giggs and David Beckham combine to put United 5-0 up at Stamford Bridge and through to the fourth round of the FA Cup. Beckham takes a short corner to Giggs, who waits for his team-mate to pass him before playing the ball back – Beckham then sends a cross into the middle and Teddy Sheringham has all the time in the world to nod home as Chelsea's miserable day continues. The hosts will actually pull three goals back in the minutes that remain as the Reds' defence switches off, much to Peter Schmeichel's chagrin.

14 February 2004

United book a spot in the FA Cup quarter-finals with a third goal without reply against Manchester City. Quinton Fortune attacks the left of the City box and drifts past Antoine Sibierski's half-hearted challenge before picking out Ryan Giggs in the middle. His shot is well saved by keeper Árni Arason, but Cristiano Ronaldo is first to react, prodding home from a couple of yards out to make it 3-0 at Old Trafford.

28 February 2010

Wayne Rooney bags the winner in the League Cup Final as United retain the trophy for the first time. Dimitar Berbatov finds Antonio Valencia on the right of the Aston Villa box and his chipped cross sees Rooney, standing on the penalty spot, generate enough power to head the ball under the crossbar and in for his 28th goal of another fantastic season and secure a 2-1 win for the Reds. It is United's fourth League Cup triumph, but the first time they have successfully defended a major cup competition and the first time any side had retained the trophy since Brian Clough's Nottingham Forest managed the feat in 1990.

75

29 August 1908

Jimmy Turnbull becomes the first player to score a hat-trick in the FA Charity Shield as he rounds off a memorable day against QPR in the replay at a packed Stamford Bridge. Charlie Roberts's fine pass out to Billy Meredith sees the Welsh winger spot Turnbull in the box and his cross is turned home by the Scottish forward to ensure the Reds take the Shield for the first time.

24 October 1956

The battle of Manchester as First Division champions United take on FA Cup winners City for the FA Charity Shield. Though the league champions usually hosted the game, as it was midweek, Maine Road had floodlights whereas Old Trafford was yet to install them. This would be the very first competitive floodlit Manchester derby, but despite a decent crowd of 30,495, it was a dull affair with Dennis Viollet grabbing the only goal of the game 15 minutes from time to ensure the Shield went back to Old Trafford rather than Maine Road.

28 November 1990

Having seen Arsenal come from 3-0 down to 3-2, United get a crucial fourth goal to derail the Gunners' recovery. Mark Hughes rides a strong tackle on the left of the box before laying the ball to his right where Denis Irwin sends in a first-time cross and Lee Sharpe gets in front of his marker before glancing a header past David Seaman to make it 4-2 in a thrilling League Cup tie at Highbury.

13 February 2005

United seal the points by going 2-0 up against Manchester City at the Etihad. Wayne Rooney had put the Reds ahead just seven minutes earlier and there are similarities between that goal and the second as Cristiano Ronaldo skips past Sylvain Distin and fires a cross towards the six-yard box from the right flank and City defender Richard Dunne, eager to get to the ball first, connects and inadvertently deflects the ball past his own keeper into the far-left corner to double the Reds' lead.

18 December 2008

Having just seen their lead halved against Gamba Osaka, United restore a two-goal advantage almost immediately. Darren Fletcher floats a ball into the path of fellow sub Wayne Rooney, who chases the pass and though he fails to control in the way he intended, he is still sharp enough to get ahead of a defender and send an angled left-foot shot past the keeper to make it 3-1 in the semi-final of the FIFA Club World Cup.

76

29 September 2001

Juan Sebastian Veron puts United 4-3 up at White Hart Lane as the Reds' incredible second-half comeback continues. Three down at the break, United are a different side after the restart and when Veron nears the left side of the Spurs box, he strikes a low, angled left-foot shot past Kasey Keller and into the bottom-right corner to stun the home fans.

17 April 2005

Game, set and match as Cristiano Ronaldo puts United 4-1 up in the FA Cup semi-final against Newcastle at the Millennium Stadium. The Magpies had pulled a goal back, but any hopes of recovering in the time that remained are ended when a swift burst forward sees Ruud van Nistelrooy receive the ball just inside the Magpies' box. He then feeds Ronaldo in space and the Portuguese winger finishes with a low shot to end the game as a contest.

21 October 2008

Wayne Rooney seals a 3-0 Champions League win over Celtic at Old Trafford. Ryan Giggs moves purposefully into the box before finding Rooney on the edge and his quick turn and low drive into the bottom-left corner from

20 yards ends the group stage clash as a contest and is his ninth goal in seven games for club and country.

8 August 2010

Javier Hernandez marks his debut with a bizarre goal in the FA Community Shield against Chelsea. The Mexican has grounds for claiming a goal – and an assist – as the Reds go 2-0 up at Wembley. John O'Shea plays a fine pass down the right flank for Antonio Valencia, who races to the side of the Chelsea box before picking out Hernandez at the far post with a low cross. As he goes to slide the ball home, he gets tangled up and the ball strikes his heel and hits him full in the face before going into the bottom-right corner.

77

12 April 2011

United score just 50 seconds after Chelsea had equalised in the Champions League quarter-final second leg at Old Trafford. It is an immediate response to Didier Drogba's equalising goal for Carlo Ancelotti's side. Ryan Giggs finds Ji-Sung Park on the left of the Chelsea box and the South Korean takes a touch before firing a low, angled shot past Petr Cech and into the bottom-right corner to make it 2-1 on the night and 3-1 on aggregate. It also means Giggs had assisted all three goals for the Reds over both ties and with no further scoring, it books a semi-final spot against Schalke.

24 November 2019

United rise from the dead to score a second goal in six minutes and make it 2-2 against Sheffield United. The home side had looked odds-on to claim three points but the Reds dig deep and when Marcus Rashford crosses from the right towards the six-yard box, Mason Greenwood is on hand to steer the ball home from close range.

78

18 May 1985

Republic of Ireland central defender Kevin Moran becomes the first player to be sent off in an FA Cup Final to leave United facing the last 11 minutes or so plus the possibility of extra time with just ten men. When Everton's Peter Reid is first to a loose ball just over the halfway line, he knocks it forward and Moran brings him down with a heavy challenge and as he's the last man, referee Peter Willis orders the defender off. An inconsolable Moran reacts furiously and has to be pulled away from the official, but the decision stands and Moran's unwanted piece of history is confirmed – though he will later join the celebrations as United win the game 1-0.

28 November 1990

Lee Sharpe completes a 33-minute hat-trick as United go 5-2 up against Arsenal at Highbury. The goal that books a place in the last 16 of the League Cup comes when Mark Hughes wins possession in his own half before finding Danny Wallace, who drives towards the Gunners' box then nudges it to his right where Sharpe hits a low shot into the bottom-left corner from 15 yards.

22 December 2001

Phil Neville joins the party as United complete a 6-1 win over Southampton at Old Trafford. Neville cuts in from the right flank and drifts easily past two defenders until he is within sight of goal where he fires a powerful shot into the left corner from 20 yards.

28 October 2003

David Bellion levels for United in the League Cup tie away to Leeds United at Elland Road. The hosts had been ahead since the 49th minute when Roque Junior headed home from a corner, but the Reds keep going and 12 minutes from time they get a deserved leveller. Having gone close just before, Bellion makes no mistake as he races on to Eric Djemba-Djemba's clever threaded through pass to drill the ball through keeper Paul Robinson's legs and ultimately force extra time.

18 December 2008

Gamba Osaka concede a third headed goal as United go 4-1 up in the semi-final of the FIFA Club World Cup. The Japanese champions are caught out again when Patrice Evra plays a neat one-two before running into space on the left. Evra then sends the ball towards the penalty spot where Darren Fletcher heads down powerfully to give the keeper no chance.

79

18 December 2008

United score a third goal in five minutes as Gamba Osaka crumble in the semi-final of the FIFA Club World Cup. This time, a move that starts on the edge of the Reds' box ends with Ryan Giggs playing a through ball to Wayne Rooney who, despite the attentions of a defender and an onrushing keeper, slips a low left-footed shot home to make it 5-1.

24 November 2019

United go from 2-0 down to 3-2 up against Sheffield United in a remarkable eight-minute turnaround. A terrific move down the left ends with Daniel James's cut-back to Marcus Rashford, who makes no mistake from close range. United will ship a late goal in spite of this to draw 3-3.

80

24 April 1948

United go ahead for the first time in the FA Cup Final against Blackpool. Having twice trailed and then twice levelled, the Reds take the lead ten minutes from time when Charlie Mitten sends in a cross from the left and Jack Rowley collects and rolls the ball to Stan Pearson, who tucks a low shot into the bottom-left corner to make it 3-2 at Wembley.

6 February 1989

Super Sub Ole Gunnar Solskjaer – a 72nd-minute replacement for Dwight Yorke – gets the first of four goals in a scintillating cameo against Nottingham Forest at the City Ground.

It's all too easy as David Beckham feeds the overlapping Gary Neville on the right of the box and his low cross finds the unmarked Solskjaer at the far post to make it 5-1.

14 February 2004

Ten-man United score a third goal in nine minutes to go 4-1 up against Kevin Keegan's Manchester City at Old Trafford. A free kick is whipped in from the right and Roy Keane at the far post manages to knock it back across the box where Ruud van Nistelrooy – almost on the goal line – can't miss to finally end City's hopes of progressing in the competition.

20 September 2009

Having waited nearly 12 months for a goal, like buses, two come along at once for Darren Fletcher. In a ding-dong Manchester derby at Old Trafford, City had twice fought back from being a goal down but their Achilles heel at crosses into the box rears its head again as Ryan Giggs crosses in from the left and Fletcher again rises higher than any City defender to expertly place the ball past Shay Given and put the Reds 3-2 up.

81

15 August 1965

United go 2-1 up in the FA Charity Shield against Liverpool at Old Trafford. In an entertaining game, neither side wants to give the other a psychological edge going into the new campaign and when David Herd scores with a typical nonchalant finish past keeper Tommy Lawrence nine minutes from time, it seems Matt Busby's men will win the game – but Liverpool level on 86 minutes to draw 2-2 and both clubs share the trophy for the 1965/66 season.

28 November 1990

United continue to run riot at Highbury with a sixth goal. Brian McClair runs at the beleaguered Gunners defence before playing the ball wide to Mark Hughes. The pass is slightly overhit, forcing Hughes to the byline where he drills a low cross towards the near post and David Seaman's fumble allows Danny Wallace the simplest of tasks to make it 6-2 as the Reds cruise into the last 16 of the League Cup.

30 August 1999

Ryan Giggs completes a 5-1 win over managerless Newcastle United at Old Trafford and proves his right foot isn't just for standing on. As four-goal Andy Cole goes looking for his fifth of the game, he plays a low ball into Giggs who attempts to return the favour – but the ball hits a defender, loops up and Giggs instinctively volleys past Tommy Wright from five yards to claim a rare right-footed goal.

14 August 1994

A spectacular overhead kick by Paul Ince seals a 2-0 victory for United over Blackburn Rovers in the FA Charity Shield. Ince, who won a penalty in the first half which was converted by Eric Cantona, is repaid by the Frenchman as Ryan Giggs's right-wing corner is nodded on by the number seven and Ince acrobatically connects with a superb bicycle kick that gives the Rovers keeper no chance from eight yards out.

22 May 2004

Ruud van Nistelrooy grabs his second goal of the FA Cup Final to seal victory over Millwall. Paul Scholes starts the move that sees Ryan Giggs drift in from the left before beating the right-back and striking a low cross/shot that van Nistelrooy slides home from a couple of yards out to make it 3-0 at the Millennium Stadium and end the game as a contest. It is the Dutch striker's 30th goal of the season and secures United's 11th FA Cup triumph.

10 April 2007

Patrice Evra provides the icing on the cake as United go 7-1 up against Roma. The Italians' humiliation is complete when an attack down the right flank sees Evra receive a pass on the edge of the box and the French full-back fires a slow shot that wrong-foots the keeper as it rolls past him and into the back of the net via the foot of the right post. It makes the score 8-3 on aggregate and wins the Reds a Champions League semi-final spot against AC Milan.

5 April 2009

Cristiano Ronaldo sets up a grandstand finish as he brings United level at 2-2 with Aston Villa. Having lost the last two games after 16 unbeaten prior to that, there seems a real danger the Reds' title challenge is coming off the rails as Villa lead 2-1 going into the final ten minutes of normal time. But United are not about to allow Liverpool to steal their crown and a neat passing move on the edge of the Villa box ends with Michael Carrick playing it to Ronaldo, who fires a low shot from 22 yards just inside the right-hand post.

21 May 2016

Having fallen behind to Crystal Palace just three minutes earlier, it looks as though United's hopes of winning their first FA Cup in 12 years are fading fast. But Wayne Rooney picks up the ball midway inside the Palace half before setting off on a mazy run that sees him go past six players before scooping a cross into the middle from the right and Marouane Fellaini chests it into the path of Juan Mata, who volleys a low shot into the bottom-left corner via a defender's leg to bring the Reds level at 1-1.

82

24 April 1948

John Anderson makes it two goals for United in the space of three minutes as they go 4-2 up to seal a second FA Cup triumph. It had been 39 years since United's last final and the mighty Blackpool represented a sizeable challenge for Matt Busby's men, but the fans from Manchester in the near-100,000 crowd celebrate as the fourth goes in – United's 98th goal of a fantastic campaign and the trophy is finally on its way back to Old Trafford.

28 August 2011

When Patrice Evra is tripped in the box, Wayne Rooney has the opportunity to cap a magnificent performance by completing his hat-trick. Rooney had been heavily involved in putting the Reds 6-1 up against Arsenal by scoring twice and making another – as well as striking the woodwork – and there is never a chance he will miss from the penalty spot as he sends Wojciech Szczęsny the wrong way to make it 7-2.

83

7 August 2016

Zlatan Ibrahimovic climbs above Wes Morgan to head home the winner of the FA Community Shield clash with Leicester City. With the game finely poised at 1-1, Antonio Valencia takes on Demarai Gray on the left of the Foxes' box, eventually taking him on for pace as he knocks it ahead and then sits up a cross into the middle where Ibrahimovic rises to head the ball past Kasper Schmeichel and in off the post to seal a 2-1 win at Wembley.

11 August 2018

A special moment for Luke Shaw, who scores his first senior career goal to put United 2-0 up against Leicester City at Old Trafford. The goal itself is not the prettiest, with Juan Mata spotting the left-back's run towards the box and lofting a pass that Shaw mis-controls, but the ball bounces over his marker and Shaw is first to react, hooking a low angled shot past Kasper Schmeichel to wrap up the points.

84

21 April 1999

United get the goal that means a place in the Champions League Final. It is fully deserved, too, with the Reds recovering from 2-0 down on 11 minutes to win 3-2 away to Juventus and 4-3 on aggregate. With the hosts chasing a goal of their own, Peter Schmeichel sends the ball upfield and Montero clears it straight to Dwight Yorke, 35 yards out. He heads for goal, jinking between Montero and Ferrara, and taking advantage of a fortuitous ricochet before rounding goalkeeper Peruzzi who trips him up – but strike partner Andy Cole is following up and races in to stroke the ball home from a tight angle and make it 3-2 as the Reds win for the first time on Italian soil.

9 December 2006

Cristiano Ronaldo finally seals victory in the Manchester derby to give the Reds a 3-1 win against City and put his side nine points clear of champions Chelsea at the top of the Premier League. City had halved the deficit through a stunning Hatem Trabelsi strike and are still very much in the game but Wayne Rooney's cross is fluffed by Richard Dunne, allowing Ronaldo a simple half-volley finish past Andreas Isaksson, though there is more than a hint of offside about the goal.

5 November 2008

United level at Parkhead to earn a 1-1 draw in the Champions League group stage clash with Celtic. The Bhoys had gone ahead with a goal on 13 minutes, but the Reds grab the equaliser when Cristiano Ronaldo's viciously swerving 25-yard shot is just about kept out by keeper Artur Boruc – but Ryan Giggs is first to the bouncing ball and nods home from a couple of yards out.

23 April 2011

Javier Hernandez keeps United on course for the title with a late winner against a dogged and determined Everton at Old Trafford. The Toffees had been resilient and managed to repel most of the Reds' attacks until former Manchester City captain Sylvain Distin gifts Antonio Valencia possession and his cross into the middle is headed home by the predatory Hernandez to make it 1-0, and ensure United stay six points clear of Chelsea with only four games to play.

15 January 2016

Zlatan Ibrahimovic rescues a deserved point for United at home to Liverpool. The visitors had led thanks to James Milner's 27th-minute penalty, but when Marouane Fellaini's header hits the post, Antonio Valencia reacts quickly to cross the ball back in and Ibrahimovic rises to head past Simon Mignolet and in off the underside of the crossbar to make it 1-1.

85

25 May 1963

David Herd scores his second goal to seal a 3-1 FA Cup Final win over Leicester City at Wembley. Keeper Gordon Banks makes a hash of a deep cross into the box, dropping the ball as he jumps to collect, and Herd can't believe his luck as it falls at his feet and he drives home to wrap up a third FA Cup triumph for the Reds.

11 August 1996

David Beckham ensures United will be collecting the FA Charity Shield as he puts the Reds 3-0 up against Newcastle United at Wembley. A quick passing move sees Eric Cantona lift the ball over the Magpies' defence for Beckham to race clear and with keeper Pavel Srnicek stranded out of his goal, the young midfielder calmly lobs it over his head and into the back of the net from 25 yards to finish the game as a contest.

7 April 2009

United get what seems to be a late winner in the Champions League round of 16 first leg against Porto. A brilliantly worked goal starts with Gary Neville's throw-in on the left of the box finding Wayne Rooney, who flicks the ball behind for Carlos Tevez to smash a shot into the roof of the net from the corner of the six-yard box to make it 2-1 with just five minutes of normal time remaining. The Portuguese will, however, grab a dramatic late goal to shift the momentum of the tie firmly in favour of the visitors ahead of the second leg.

86

7 February 1970

That rarest of rare beasts – a double hat-trick – is completed by the irrepressible George Best to put United 8-1 up against Northampton Town at the County Ground. If the home fans in the 21,771 crowd had come in the hope of seeing Best in action, they weren't disappointed as he rounds off a virtuoso performance with his sixth goal of the FA Cup fifth-round tie. Paddy Crerand plays a low pass across the edge of the Cobblers' box and Best collects, moves forward, shimmies to set the keeper on his backside before rolling the ball into the net and setting a new Manchester United goal-scoring feat in the process.

10 April 1993

In a game that will go down in United folklore, Steve Bruce heads home from a corner to make it 1-1 with Sheffield Wednesday. The Reds' march towards a first Premier League title had been stuttering and dropping points against the Owls was not an option, so the relief is palpable as the ball comes into the box from the right and Bruce – from almost the edge of the box – somehow generates enough power to send the ball into the top-left corner to set up a grandstand finish at Old Trafford.

13 May 2009

Michael Carrick strikes a superb late winner to put United within a point of an 18th league title. The Reds had gone toe-to-toe with Liverpool all season but were behind to Wigan Athletic up to the hour. Then, Carlos Tevez equalised and it is Carrick who makes it 2-1, sending a sizzling left-footed drive into the top-left corner from the edge of the Wigan box to send the 6,000-plus travelling United fans into ecstasy.

7 November 2008

Juan Mata scores a superb free kick to seemingly rescue a vital point for United against Juventus. United are awarded a free kick on the edge of the box, Ashley Young runs towards the ball but steps over it and Mata quickly follows, curling a left-footed shot over the wall and into the top-left corner to make it 1-1 – though the Reds weren't quite finished yet.

17 October 2020

A brilliant, sweeping United counter attack ends with a stunning finish from Bruno Fernandes as the Reds go 2-1 up away to Newcastle. Donny van de Beek starts the move with a neat one-two deep inside United's half. Juan Mata receives a pass and plays a ball into the Magpies' half for Marcus Rashford, who drives forward into the box before cleverly disguising his reverse pass to Fernandes, who takes one touch before curling a shot into the top-right corner from a tight angle.

87

4 March 1995

Andy Cole scores his fifth goal of the game as United complete the 9-0 rout of Ipswich Town at Old Trafford. Ryan Giggs's corner from the left sees Paul Ince leap to head down to the waiting Cole who, with his back to goal, spins around and fires a fierce shot into the top-right corner to complete an unforgettable afternoon and finally end the Tractor Boys' misery. The United fans shout 'We want ten!' while the Ipswich supporters respond with 'We want one!'

The scoreline sets a new Premier League record that Leicester City would equal in 2019 and the Reds repeat in 2021 – with Southampton on the end of both of those two thrashings.

11 August 1996

Roy Keane ensures United's 1996/97 campaign starts in perfect style as he makes it 4-0 against Kevin Keegan's Newcastle United in the FA Charity Shield at Wembley. It's a stunning strike from the Irishman, too, as Ryan Giggs rolls a free kick on the left of the Magpies' box across to the unmarked Keane 20 yards out and his rising shot beats the keeper and flies into the roof of the net to complete the rout.

29 September 2001

David Beckham completes United's thrilling comeback by scoring a fifth second-half goal against Spurs. Any hopes the punch-drunk hosts had of at least recovering to grab a late draw are ended when the England skipper receives the ball slightly right of the D on the edge of the box. He tees himself up before firing an arrow-like shot past Kasey Keller into the right of the net to make it 5-3. An incredible comeback from a side that trailed 3-0 at half-time.

24 November 2010

Wayne Rooney ends Rangers' hopes of Champions League progress as he converts what will be the only goal of the game at Ibrox. In the group stage clash against the Scottish champions, Steven Naismith's high challenge on Fabio da Silva is adjudged to be dangerous play and the ref points to the spot. Rooney sends Allan McGregor the wrong way to seal a 1-0 win for the Reds.

29 February 2017

Having seen a 2-0 lead wiped out by Southampton, who score either side of half-time and also hit the woodwork, Zlatan Ibrahimovic has the final say with the winning goal just three minutes from the end of normal time in the League Cup Final. The Saints defence seems to switch off as Ander Herrera has the ball on the right of the box and his dinked cross picks out Ibrahimovic for a fairly simple headed goal to give José Mourinho's men a 3-2 victory and a fifth League Cup triumph.

2 February 2021

When Anthony Martial is pulled down as he goes past Jan Bednarek, the referee has an easy decision to award a penalty – he also shows Bednarek a straight red card to reduce the Saints to nine men. Bruno Fernandes adds to the punishment as he sends Alex McCarthy the wrong way to make it 7-0 in the Premier League clash at Old Trafford.

88

6 February 1989

Ole Gunnar Solskjaer gets his second goal of the game to put the Reds 6-1 up against Ron Atkinson's Nottingham Forest. The shambolic Forest defence allow David Beckham to pick out the Norwegian's clever run and with just Dave Beasant to beat, he tries an impudent chip that the keeper blocks on the edge of the box, but it falls back to Solskjaer who then takes it around Beasant before thumping a powerful shot into the net from 15 yards.

17 March 1999

With United 1-0 down and clinging on against Inter Milan in the second leg of the Champions League quarter-final, Paul Scholes gets the goal that finally kills off the Italians' hopes. The Reds had won the first leg 2-0 but a second-half onslaught by Inter had seen then score and go close to getting a second on several occasions – but when Andy Cole cushions a deep cross from the right down to the feet of Scholes, he makes no mistake from seven yards to make it 1-1 on the night and 3-1 on aggregate.

24 January 1999

United finally get the goal they so richly deserve against Liverpool in the FA Cup fourth round at Old Trafford.

Trailing to a first-half Michael Owen goal, the Reds are denied time and time again until finally a David Beckham free kick finds Andy Cole at the far post and his header down is bundled home from a yard or so out to make it 1-1.

22 August 1999

Roy Keane settles a bad-tempered Premier League clash against Arsenal at Highbury with a goal two minutes from time. Keane and Patrick Vieira could easily have seen red for a violent altercation in the second half, and both would have a part to play in the game's decisive goal. Vieira showboats somewhat on the left of his own half before pinging a high pass to Dennis Bergkamp who nods the ball back to Ray Parlour, but his attempt to nutmeg Ryan Giggs sees the United winger race forward and fire a shot at goal. That shot is deflected into the path of Keane, who chests the ball down before tucking it neatly past the keeper from eight yards for his second of the game and to put United 2-1 up.

23 December 2020

Edinson Cavani grabs a late winner for United away to Everton. In front of just 2,000 fans because of restrictions driven by the COVID-19 pandemic, the Uruguayan puts the Reds into the League Cup semi-final after Anthony Martial's incisive pass to feet allows Cavani to skip inside a challenge before firing a powerful low shot into the bottom-left corner and putting United 1-0 up at Goodison Park.

89

6 March 1966

Bobby Charlton put the icing on the cake as United humble Portuguese giants Benfica on their own ground. Already leading 4-1 and heading for the European Cup semi-final, an intricate team move sees the ball flicked to Charlton on the edge of the Benfica box and the United and England legend collects before waltzing past a couple of half-hearted challenges, walking around the keeper and rolling the ball into the empty net to make it 5-1 on the night and 8-3 on aggregate.

21 April 1993

On an evening when United will end their 26-year wait for a top-flight title, Paul Ince scores to wrap up a 2-0 victory away to Crystal Palace. Eric Cantona's delightful chip from the left picks out Ince in the middle and he then drives into the box before sending a low shot past the keeper from ten yards.

90

6 February 1989

Ole Gunnar Solskjaer completes a ten-minute hat-trick off the bench as hapless Nottingham Forest concede a seventh at the City Ground. Paul Scholes plays a neat one-two midway inside the Forest half before lofting a chipped pass to the unmarked Solskjaer, who controls the ball before volleying home from 12 yards to ensure the match ball is his and put United 7-1 up.

3 May 1993

Gary Pallister scores his first goal for 18 months on a celebratory afternoon with United having been confirmed Premier League champions for the first time in 26 years. When a free kick is awarded on the edge of the Blackburn Rovers box, Pallister looks the least likely candidate to take it but the central defender clearly fancies it so runs up and strikes a low shot through the wall and into the bottom-right corner to make it 3-1 and get the title party really started.

24 January 1999

Pandemonium at Old Trafford as Ole Gunnar Solskjaer makes it two goals in three minutes to turn the FA Cup fourth round tie with Liverpool on its head. Just a few minutes earlier, the Reds were staring at a 1-0 defeat at Old Trafford but when the ball is chipped into the Liverpool box, Paul Scholes manages to get a touch that diverts it into Solskjaer's path and his low shot wrong-foots the keeper and goes into the back of the net to make it 2-1 and win the tie in a breathless finish between the two old adversaries.

25 February 2001

Teddy Sheringham completes the rout of Arsenal as he makes it 6-1 in the last minute. Gary Neville dinks a ball to Sheringham on the edge of the Gunners' box and he cushions a header to Solskjaer, who cuts inside a challenge but before he can shoot, Sheringham races in to sweep a low shot past David Seaman. It was the Reds' first goal for some 52 minutes having led 5-1 since the 38th minute and it puts Alex's men 16 points clear at the top of the Premier League.

27 April 2003

Ruud van Nistelrooy seals the victory that will put United five points clear of Arsenal at the top of the Premier League with only three games to play. With just seconds of normal time remaining, Quinton Fortune bursts forward through a couple of challenges and into the Spurs half before spotting van Nistelrooy on the edge of the box. He drifts a ball over two defenders into the Dutchman's path and after taking one touch to tee himself up, the prolific striker drills a low shot past the keeper to wrap up a crucial three points and edge United towards yet another title.

17 January 2009

With United scoring the winning goal in the first minute of their previous game against Wigan, it is only fitting that Dimitar Berbatov should score in the final minute of the next game. Away to Bolton Wanderers, the Reds score the only goal as Carlos Tevez's fine cross is headed home by Berbatov for the Reds to go top of the Premier League for the first time in the 2008/09 campaign.

7 November 2008

United – who had trailed 1-0 with five minutes of the Champions League group stage clash with Juventus in Turin – make it two goals in five minutes to complete a stunning turnaround against the Old Lady. The winner is as untidy as they come, with Marouane Fellaini getting a slight flick on an Ashley Young free kick from the left and a combination of Juve's Leonardo Bonucci and Alex Sandro bundling the ball over the line at the far post to give the Reds a stunning 2-1 win.

17 October 2020

A big moment for Aaron Wan-Bissaka as United wrap up three points at St James' Park. After running on to a pass from Marcus Rashford, Wan-Bissaka thumps a right-footed shot into the roof of the net from 15 yards to put the Reds 3-1 up against Newcastle. It is also Wan-Bissaka's first goal in professional football – what a way to open your account.

2 February 2021

More woeful defending by nine-man Southampton allows United to go 8-0 up. Reds players are queuing up as Aaron Wan-Bissaka send in a fine cross from the right of the Saints box and Anthony Martial has time to chest the ball down and volley home unchallenged as the visitors' evening gets even worse – though it is not quite finished.

Added Time

90+1

6 February 1989

United's destruction of Nottingham Forest is complete as the rampant Reds go 8-1 up at the City Ground. And it's a fourth goal in just 11 minutes for substitute Ole Gunnar Solskjaer. Nicky Butt's low cross from the right finds Paul Scholes whose shot is blocked, but only a yard to the left where Solskjaer gets the ball under control and then makes no mistake from seven yards. Three of his four goals had come in just four minutes.

26 May 1999

Having been behind for 85 minutes of the Champions League Final, United fans are resigned to losing to Bayern Munich at the Camp Nou in Barcelona. With Peter Schmeichel coming up for a corner, David Beckham crosses into the box where the ball is only half-cleared to Ryan Giggs who mis-hits a low shot that goes to sub Teddy Sheringham, who gets enough on the ball to send it into the bottom-right corner to make it 1-1 and seemingly earn the Reds another 30 minutes of extra time – but the drama wasn't quite finished yet.

MANCHESTER UNITED: MINUTE BY MINUTE

21 September 2003

Ugly scenes as United are awarded a penalty in added time against Arsenal at Old Trafford. With the score 0-0 in an early-season meeting between the two teams most likely to challenge for the title, Diego Forlan goes down under the challenge of Martin Keown in the box and the referee points to the spot. Ruud van Nistelrooy, who had been the target of the Arsenal players' anger when Partick Vieira was sent off for a challenge on the Dutchman ten minutes earlier, steps up to take the penalty, but he smacks his shot against the crossbar.

The final whistle goes moments later and the Arsenal players lose their cool, surrounding van Nistelrooy like a pack of dogs, pushing him and shouting in his face. The game ends 0-0, but the over-reaction at the end of the game leaves a sour taste.

24 April 2007

United grab a crucial first-leg lead against AC Milan in a dramatic and thrilling Champions League semi-final at Old Trafford. In a see-saw battle between the best teams in the Premier League and Serie A, United had led, then trailed before finally winning the game in added time. Ryan Giggs lays a clever ball into the path of Rooney on the right of the Milan box and Rooney's immediate shot catches the keeper off guard as it rifles into the bottom-right corner to give the Reds a narrow but deserved 3-2 lead to take into the second leg in Italy.

6 December 2008

Nemanja Vidic spares United's blushes with an added-time winner against managerless Sunderland at Old Trafford. The Reds had already struck the woodwork twice but had otherwise been denied by an inspired goalkeeping performance by Black Cats keeper Marton Fulop – but even he can't keep out Vidic's last-gasp winner, with the burly defender turning home from close range to give the Reds a 1-0 victory after Michael Carrick's shot had come to him via the post.

28 August 2011

The perfect end to the perfect day for the rampant Reds. In the first minute of added time, Ashley Young picks up the ball on the left of the Arsenal box, from where he curls a sublime shot into the top-right corner from 20 yards – his second cracker of the game – and completes an 8-2 win over the hapless north Londoners, who had been close to shambolic. It is the first time the Gunners have shipped eight goals since 1896.

27 November 2018

Marouane Fellaini grabs a priceless added-time goal to give United a 1-0 Champions League group stage win over Young Boys. The Reds had failed to score against Valencia (0-0) and Juventus (0-1) in the previous two home group games and looked to be heading for a painful goalless draw with the struggling Swiss side until Luke Shaw's cross is flicked on by Romelu Lukaku and Fellaini holds off Loris Benito and fires into the bottom corner, much to the relief of José Mourinho and the 72,876 crowd. The victory guarantees United a place in the round of 16.

90+2

14 May 1994

The icing on the cake as United complete a Premier League and FA Cup double in style by going 4-0 up against Chelsea in the 1994 FA Cup Final. The fourth goal is the pick of the bunch, too, with Eric Cantona playing a ball into Mark Hughes from the right flank and Hughes then threads Paul Ince through on goal. Ince takes it around Dmitri Kharine before unselfishly squaring past the lone defender in front of him to allow Brian McClair to tap into the empty net.

7 April 1999

Ryan Giggs sends Old Trafford wild with a superb close-range half-volley into the roof of the net to give the Reds a vital lifeline in the Champions League semi-final against Juventus. The Italian giants had led 1-0 from Antonio Conte's first-half goal but a stoppage-time melee sees the ball fall to Giggs, who makes no mistake from six yards to give the Reds some hope going into the second leg.

9 August 2009

Wayne Rooney levels to force a penalty shoot-out in the FA Community Shield against Chelsea. Trailing 2-1 with just seconds remaining, Ryan Giggs controls a high ball and then plays a suspiciously offside-looking Rooney clear and the United striker tucks a low shot past Petr Cech into the bottom-right corner to make it 2-2 – though the Reds will lose 4-1 on spot-kicks to the west Londoners.

27 January 2010

Old Trafford goes crazy as United get the goal that means a Wembley date in the League Cup Final after a pulsating all-Manchester semi-final against City. With the aggregate score level at 3-3 it looks as though extra time will be needed to determine the winner, but the Reds make one last attempt to settle the game in normal time and when Ryan Giggs's cross comes in towards the six-yard box, the ball clears the head of Joleon Lescott and Wayne Rooney heads home from close range to give Shay Given no chance, making it 3-1 on the night and 4-3 on aggregate and settle the tie.

8 August 2010

A typically classy finish by Dimitar Berbatov seals a 3-1 FA Community Shield victory for United at Wembley. With Chelsea pushing for a late equaliser, Nani impudently flicks the ball to Berbatov, putting him clear on goal and as Petr Cech races out, he casually lifts the ball over his head and into the net from the edge of the box. A sublime finish from a player who made everything look effortless.

9 December 2012

United snatch a dramatic winner to triumph 3-2 in the top-of-the-table Manchester derby clash at the Etihad. City had fought back from 2-0 down to level the scores and the game seems to be heading towards a draw when Carlos Tevez ankle taps Rafael on the right of the Blues' box. Robin van Persie and Wayne Rooney stand over the ball but it is the Dutch striker who runs up and strikes a curling left foot shot that catches a wafting leg of Samir Nasri and takes it away from the dive of Joe Hart to give the Reds a dramatic win. It is all the more galling for City fans because van Persie had chosen to go to United rather than City in the summer as the Manchester clubs entered a tug-of-war for the Arsenal star.

90+3

26 May 1999

In the final minute of added time in the 1999 Champions League Final, United complete the most incredible comeback you will see in a major final. Having trailed 1-0 going into time added on for stoppages, Teddy Sheringham levelled to send the United fans inside the Camp Nou wild. Nobody could have guessed that two minutes later, the Reds would score again, but that's what happens as David Beckham's corner finds Sheringham in the six-yard box and his flicked header is instinctively prodded into the roof of the net by fellow sub Ole Gunnar Solskjaer to make it 2-1. With just seconds remaining, the Reds fans in the 90,245 crowd celebrate with a touch of disbelief. In the space of three minutes, Alex Ferguson's men had gone from losing the final to winning it and completing an unprecedented treble of Champions League, Premier League and FA Cup. It is also the first time in 31 years that the Reds are crowned European champions.

5 April 2009

United grab the added-time winner that ensures the Premier League title race takes a dramatic twist in their favour. Having looked like suffering a third straight defeat at a crucial stage of the campaign, United dig deep to score the winning goal as Ryan Giggs feeds Italian teenager Federico Macheda just inside the box on the left. Macheda cleverly turns his marker from left to right as he spins and curls a superb shot into the far-left corner to make it 3-2 and send Old Trafford wild.

27 April 2010

Paul Scholes does what he has done throughout his illustrious career as he times a run to perfection to head home and settle the Manchester derby deep into added time. Drawing 0-0 with City at the Etihad but needing three points to stay on track for the title, the Reds launch one final attack, with Scholes involved in the move as the ball is worked out to the left where Patrice Evra is in plenty of space. The French left-back looks up and chips a ball in towards the penalty spot where Scholes runs on to power a header into the bottom-right corner.

23 April 2016

With just seconds remaining of added time before extra time is needed to determine a victor, Louis van Gaal's United grab a dramatic winner to make the score 2-1 against Everton and settle the FA Cup semi-final at Wembley. The move that leads to the goal starts with skipper Wayne Rooney, who plays the ball out to Anthony Martial on the left and the French forward brings the ball inside, playing a one-two with Marcus Rashford. He then tries the same with Ander Herrera and the Spaniard just about manages to scramble a return pass that allows Martial to run into the box before placing a low shot into the bottom-right corner, sending the Reds to the final in the process.

29 December 2020

United snatch a dramatic victory in the closing moments against Wolves to end 2020 with three points. Marcus Rashford picks up the ball on the far right of the Wolves box before cutting inside, patiently taking on a defender and working a yard of space. He fires a left-footed shot that strikes Romain Saiss on its way past a wrong-footed Rui Patricio to give the Reds a 1-0 victory at Old Trafford.

2 February 2021

United complete their rout of Southampton in added time with a ninth goal. Mason Greenwood floats a ball to the back post where Bruno Fernandes heads down into the middle and Dan James nonchalantly flicks the cross home past the keeper and a defender on the line as the nine-man Saints lose 9-0 for the second time in two years. The Reds record their biggest victory since thrashing Ipswich Town by the same score some 26 years previously.

90+4

7 August 2011

United complete a fantastic second-half comeback against Manchester City in one of the best FA Community Shield clashes at Wembley in living memory. Having recovered from two goals down at the break, the Reds – keen to lay an early marker down against the side Sir Alex Ferguson named the 'noisy neighbours' – snatch a dramatic winner right at the end of added time. A City attack is hacked clear and as Gael Clichy and Vincent Kompany hesitate to go for the ball, Nani nips in and races clear before rounding Joe Hart and rolling the ball into the empty net in front of the ecstatic United fans to secure a 3-2 win.

6 March 2019

A dramatic finish to a thrilling performance as United win a penalty in added time away to Paris St Germain.

The Reds had been largely written off after losing the first leg 2-0 at Old Trafford, but when Diogo Dalot's speculative shot hits Presnel Kimpembe on the arm, and after a lengthy check, the VAR declares the incident to be a deliberate act and awards a spot-kick. Ice cool Marcus Rashford steps up to score, making it 3-1 and sending United into the quarter-finals on away goals. The Reds are also the first team to successfully overturn a 2-0 (or greater) first-leg home loss in the competition's history.

90+5

25 September 2018

Ten-man United rescue a League Cup third round tie that looked to be going Derby County's way. With the Reds seeing Sergio Romero dismissed for handling the ball outside his box, Frank Lampard's side look to have won the game with an 85th-minute goal – but in United's last attack, deep into added time, Diogo Dalot sends a deep cross into the box and Marouane Fellaini rises at the far post to head the ball and though the keeper gets a good hand on it, he can only push the Belgian's effort into the roof of the net as the Reds force a penalty shoot-out at Old Trafford.

16 March 2019

Marcus Rashford scores in the dying embers of the FA Cup quarter-final with Wolves at Molineux. Luke Shaw finds Rashford with a low cross from the left of the box and Rashford takes a touch before dispatching a low shot past Rui Patricio – but it's too little, too late, with the Reds already trailing 2-0 and the hosts hold on to move into the semi-finals for the first time in 21 years.

90+6

10 April 1993

Steve Bruce goes into the history books as he heads home United's winner against Sheffield Wednesday. The centre-back looked to have rescued a point with his header on 86 minutes but he scores a second to send Old Trafford crazy, deep into added time. When Ryan Giggs's cross from the left is cleared out to the right of the Owls' box, Gary Pallister chases it and then sends the ball in – a Wednesday head gets there first but only loops it to around the penalty spot where Bruce meets it full-on to head into the left of the net and win the game 2-1, sparking joyous scenes on and off the pitch.

20 September 2009

To Manchester City's credit, Mark Hughes's side more than played their part in this thrilling derby at Old Trafford. Three times the Blues came back after falling behind and Hughes is understandably perplexed when, with the referee having indicated four minutes of added time, United launch one final attack in the sixth additional minute. Ryan Giggs – already with two assists – claims a hat-trick of setting his team-mates up as he receives the ball 30 yards from goal, spots Michael Owen in space on the left and plays in a low pass that the former Liverpool and England striker takes one touch to control before dinking a shot past Shay Given to send Old Trafford delirious and seal a 4-3 victory. It is the last kick of the game and former Reds legend Hughes is less than impressed with the officials' timekeeping.

8 March 2020

A stunning late goal seals three points and almost blows the roof off Old Trafford in the process. In a tense Manchester derby, the Blues are looking for an equaliser with the Reds leading through Anthony Martial's first-half strike. Ederson had partially been to blame for that goal, allowing the France international's shot to squeeze underneath his dive, and the Brazilian caps his miserable afternoon deep into added time as he collects the ball and then throws it towards Benjamin Mendy from the corner of his own box – but the pace on the throw gives the City left-back no chance and instead falls to Scott McTominay, who hits a first-time shot with pace, beating Ederson who had still not got back to his line and completing a 2-0 win over the defending Premier League champions.

17 October 2020

United go 4-1 up against Newcastle at St James' Park – despite the score being 1-1 just ten minutes previously. The fourth goal is no more than the icing on the cake as Bruno Fernandes plays an excellent chip from his own half behind the Magpies' defence for Marcus Rashford to run on to – he darts into the box, coming in from the left, before drilling a low shot into the bottom-right corner.

23 December 2020

Anthony Martial ensures there is no way back for Everton in the League Cup quarter-final at Goodison Park. Edinson Cavani had bagged a late goal on 88 minutes but, deep into added time, Martial doubles the Reds' lead as he runs on to Marcus Rashford's through ball to drill a low shot past Jordan Pickford and make it 2-0 with almost the last kick of the game.

90+10

26 September 2020

High drama on the south coast as United are awarded a penalty – after the final whistle had blown at the Amex against Brighton & Hove Albion. With what seems to be the last action of the game, a deep corner finds the head of Harry Maguire and as he nods the ball towards goal, it is cleared off the line with Maguire furiously appealing for a penalty. The referee blows for full time as the United players continue their appeals – and then VAR confirms Neil Maupay's raised arm brushed the ball so a spot-kick is given. Bruno Fernandes strikes the penalty into the top-right corner to give the Reds a most dramatic 3-2 win in what had been an extraordinary end to the game.

Extra Time

92

29 May 1968

United go 2-1 up against Benfica in the European Cup Final with a magical goal from George Best. Alex Stepney's long kick upfield is nodded on by Brian Kidd and Best does the rest by collecting the ball and wriggling through a couple of challenges before rounding the keeper and walking the ball into the back of the net as Matt Busby's side re-take the lead against the Portuguese giants. Brilliant by the Northern Irish genius on the biggest platform in club football.

8 April 1990

United take the lead again in the FA Cup semi-final derby with Oldham Athletic at Maine Road. With just two minutes of extra time on the clock, Brian McClair plays Danny Wallace clear and the diminutive winger takes one touch before scuffing a low shot past the onrushing keeper which sees the ball trickle just inside the right post to put the Reds 3-2 up – though the Second Division side will later level to earn a replay.

94

29 May 1968

Wembley goes wild as United make it two goals in three minutes to take a 3-1 lead over Benfica in the European Cup Final. As David Sadler heads a corner across the box, Brian Kidd gets his head on it and sees his effort cleared off the line – but only as far as Kidd himself, who then heads the ball goalwards again and this time it sails over the defender on the line, brushing the underside of the bar on its way in to put Matt Busby's side on course for a first European trophy – and quite a way for Kidd to celebrate his 19th birthday.

95

11 August 2020

Bruno Fernandes scores the goal that sends United into the Europa League semi-final with an extra-time penalty. The spot-kick – United's 21st of the season in all competitions – is awarded when Anthony Martial works his way into the box before seeing his shot saved by FC Copenhagen keeper Johnsson and as Juan Mata plays the loose ball back to Martial, Andreas Bjelland's clumsy challenge results in a foul and Fernandes confidently dispatches the spot-kick into the top corner to give the Reds a 1-0 lead in the one-off tie held in Cologne.

97

9 February 2021

Scott McTominay settles a tightly contested FA Cup fifth round tie at Old Trafford against West Ham with the only goal of the game. The teams had batted out a 0-0 draw in normal time, but with no FA Cup replays during the 2020/21 season, the match must be settled on the night and McTominay scores after a goalmouth scramble that eventually sees Marcus Rashford tee up the Scot inside the box and his low shot into the bottom corner gives the keeper no chance whatsoever.

99

29 May 1968

Bobby Charlton seals a 4-1 win over Benfica as United become European champions for the first time. The Reds score a third goal in eight minutes to destroy the Portuguese champions at Wembley. The fourth goal comes when Brian Kidd – who had already assisted one and scored another – attacks on the right of the Benfica penalty area and his low cross is brilliantly converted by Charlton, who hits a powerful angled shot from the right of the six-yard box into the top-left corner of the net for his second of the game and to seal an historic night for the Reds.

28 October 2003

Diego Forlan puts the Reds ahead for the first time against Leeds United at Elland Road. The hosts had just been denied a penalty at the other end when Forlan picks up the ball, plays it to Darren Fletcher in the box and Fletcher's return low cross is turned home by Forlan to put United 2-1 up in the League Cup third round tie.

107

20 April 2017

Marcus Rashford gets the goal that puts United into the Europa League semi-final with a neatly taken strike against Anderlecht. The Belgians had pushed United all the way, drawing the first leg 1-1 and drawing 1-1 in 90 minutes at Old Trafford but when a long ball is pumped into the Anderlecht box, Marouane Fellaini gets up to nod the ball down to the feet of Rashford on the edge of the box – and with two defenders in front of him, he shifts the ball to his left and drills a low shot home to make it 2-1 and win the tie.

109

14 April 1999

United – somehow – survived normal time against Arsenal to force extra time in the FA Cup semi-final replay against Arsenal at Villa Park. The Reds had gone ahead in the first half through David Beckham. but the Gunners finished strongly and after Dennis Bergkamp's deflected equaliser, the Reds were reduced to ten men when Roy Keane was given a second yellow card – then Nicolas Anelka saw what he thought was a late winner disallowed for offside and, even more incredibly, Peter Schmeichel then saved a Bergkamp penalty with almost the last kick of normal time. If ever there was a game that the Reds were destined to win, it was this one and when a misplaced Arsenal pass finds Ryan Giggs ten yards inside his own half, the Welsh winger runs forward, skipping past one challenge until he has four Gunners players around him on the edge of the box – he somehow tricks his way past all of them before rifling an angled shot into the roof of the net to make it 2-1 and send United to Wembley. It is an incredible individual goal and is followed by the famous run down the side of the pitch with his shirt swinging around his head.

110

18 May 1985

Ron Atkinson's ten-man United grab a dramatic winner in extra time to seal a famous FA Cup Final win over Everton. Having had Kevin Moran sent off, the Reds were up against it as legs tired on the sapping Wembley surface. Then, Norman Whiteside picks the ball up on the right wing before moving towards the Everton box and as the left-back waits for a cross, Whiteside curls an angled shot with his left foot past Neville Southall and into the bottom-left corner to make it 1-0 – a scoreline that United cling on to in order to win the trophy for the third time in eight years.

21 May 2016

A stunning way to win any game, let alone the FA Cup Final as ten-man United go 2-1 up in extra time against Crystal Palace. The Reds had trailed 1-0 with nine minutes to go before levelling, then saw Chris Smalling sent off for a second bookable offence – but still rise to the challenge and seal victory with a volley as good as you will ever see. Antonio Valencia manages to get past Jason Puncheon before sending a low cross in from the right and a Palace boot gets there first to send the ball to the edge of the box, where Jesse Lingard instantly volleys a howitzer of a shot into the top-left corner before the Palace keeper can even move. A wonderful goal.

113

12 May 1990

Mark Hughes rescues a 3-3 draw for United with an equaliser in the second half of extra time. Crystal Palace had come from 2-1 down to lead 3-2 in the 1990 FA Cup Final but Hughes scores his second of the game as Paul Ince nudges a through ball to the Welsh striker and he hits a low shot past the keeper from just inside the box into the bottom-left corner to earn the Reds a Wembley replay.

114

11 April 1990

Mark Robins climbs off the bench to score the goal that sends United to Wembley. The Reds had been taken to extra time in the FA Cup semi-final replay at Maine Road by Joe Royle's giant-killing Oldham Athletic, but Robins has the final say as Mike Phelan plays a ball towards him with the Reds counter-attacking. After teeing himself up, Robins hits a low shot that beats the keeper and just goes inside the left post to make it 2-1 and seal a place in the final against Crystal Palace, who had surprisingly beaten Liverpool at Villa Park a few days before.

117

28 October 2003

Eric Djemba-Djemba scores a dramatic late extra-time winner to give United a 3-2 victory away to Leeds United in a thrilling League Cup tie at Elland Road. A corner on the left comes all the way to Djemba-Djemba just inside the Leeds box and his first-time shot hits the turf before looping up and over keeper Paul Robinson to put the Reds into round four.

118

27 June 2020

Harry Maguire scrambles home the winner in extra time against Norwich City at Carrow Road to send the Reds into the FA Cup semi-final. The struggling Canaries, reduced to ten men just before the end of normal time, had fought valiantly until Maguire forces the ball home from close range after the hosts had failed to clear a cross into the six-yard box.

119

25 October 2007

Sub Kieran Lee saves United's blushes in a League Cup third round tie away to Crewe Alexandra. The Railwaymen had deservedly taken the Reds to extra time at Gresty Road and the game looked to be heading for a penalty shoot-out when Alan Smith slid Lee clear and the teenager made no mistake with a confident finish to give his team a 2-1 win – it will be Lee's only goal for United.

120

120

21 May 1983

The famous 'and Smith must score' moment as Brighton & Hove Albion – recently relegated from the First Division – break forward in the last minute of the 1983 FA Cup Final. With the score at 2-2, former Manchester City striker Michael Robinson chases a through pass from Jimmy Case and outmuscles Kevin Moran before laying the ball to his right where Gordon Smith only has Gary Bailey to beat, but the Seagulls forward hits a low shot straight at Bailey as radio commentator Peter Jones utters his immortal line. Smith doesn't and United survive for a replay.

120+1

22 January 2014

Javier Hernandez keeps United's hopes of taking on City in an all-Manchester League Cup Final at Wembley with a last-gasp extra-time winner against Sunderland in the semi-final second leg at Old Trafford. The Reds had lost the first leg 2-1 at the Stadium of Light but are being held 1-1 in added time at the end of extra time when Adnan Januzaj manages to cross from the left of the six-yard box and Javier Hernandez finishes powerfully from a few yards out to make it 2-1 and force a penalty shoot-out – one that United will lose 2-1.

Penalties

7 August 1993

The FA Charity Shield between United and Arsenal ends 1-1 after normal time at Wembley. With the Shield no longer shared between teams in the event of a draw, a penalty shoot-out is needed to settle the result.

- Nigel Winterburn (Arsenal) scores – 1-0
- Paul Ince (Manchester United) scores – 1-1
- John Jensen (Arsenal) scores – 2-1
- Steve Bruce (Manchester United) scores – 2-2
- Kevin Campbell (Arsenal) scores – 3-2
- Denis Irwin (Manchester United) misses – 3-2
- Paul Merson (Arsenal) scores – 4-2
- Roy Keane (Manchester United) scores – 4-3
- Ian Wright (Arsenal) misses – 4-3
- Eric Cantona (Manchester United) scores – 4-4
- David Seaman (Arsenal) misses – 4-4
- Bryan Robson (Manchester United) scores – 4-5

Manchester United win 5-4 on penalties

3 August 1997

When the 1997 FA Charity Shield ends 1-1, United and Chelsea are forced to go to a penalty shoot-out at Wembley.

- Frank Sinclair (Chelsea) misses – 0-0
- Paul Scholes (Manchester United) scores – 0-1
- Gianfranco Zola (Chelsea) scores – 1-1
- Denis Irwin (Manchester United) scores – 1-2
- Roberto Di Matteo (Chelsea) misses – 1-2
- Roy Keane (Manchester United) scores – 1-3
- Frank Leboeuf (Chelsea) scores – 2-3
- Nicky Butt (Manchester United) scores – 2-4

Manchester United win 4-2 on penalties

10 August 2003

United and Arsenal end the FA Charity Shield 1-1 at the Millennium Stadium in Cardiff. Both sides score in the first half but there are no further goals in the South Wales sunshine, meaning a penalty shoot-out is needed to separate these two modern-day rivals.

- Paul Scholes (Manchester United) scores – 1-0
- Edu (Arsenal) scores – 1-1
- Rio Ferdinand (Manchester United) scores – 2-1
- Giovanni van Bronckhorst (Arsenal) misses – 2-1
- Ruud van Nistelrooy (Manchester United) misses – 2-1
- Sylvain Wiltord (Arsenal) scores – 2-2
- Ole Gunnar Solskjaer (Manchester United) scores 3-2
- Lauren (Arsenal) scores – 3-3
- Diego Forlan (Manchester United) scores – 4-3
- Robert Pires (Arsenal) misses – 4-3

Manchester United win 4-3 on penalties

5 August 2007

After United come from behind to force a 1-1 draw with Chelsea, the FA Community Shield goes to penalties at Wembley.

- Claudio Pizarro (Chelsea) misses – 0-0
- Rio Ferdinand (Manchester United) scores – 0-1
- Frank Lampard (Chelsea) misses – 0-1
- Michael Carrick (Manchester United) scores – 0-2
- Shaun Wright-Phillips (Chelsea) misses – 0-2
- Wayne Rooney (Manchester United) scores – 0-3

Manchester United win 3-0 on penalties

21 May 2008

United and Chelsea were level at 1-1 after normal time in the 2008 Champions League Final in Moscow and after neither side scored in the ensuing 30 minutes of extra time, a penalty shoot-out had to take place to decide the next champions of Europe.

- Carlos Tevez (Manchester United) scores – 1-0
- Michael Ballack (Chelsea) scores – 1-1
- Michael Carrick (Manchester United) scores – 2-1
- Juliano Belletti (Chelsea) scores – 2-2
- Cristiano Ronaldo (Manchester United) misses – 2-2
- Frank Lampard (Chelsea) scores – 2-3
- Owen Hargreaves (Manchester United) scores – 3-3
- Ashley Cole (Chelsea) scores – 3-4
- Nani (Manchester United) scores – 4-4
- John Terry (Chelsea) misses – 4-4
- Anderson (Manchester United) scores – 5-4
- Salomon Kalou (Chelsea) scores – 5-5
- Ryan Giggs (Manchester United) scores – 6-5
- Nicolas Anelka (Chelsea) misses – 6-5

Manchester United win 6-5 on penalties

10 August 2008

Premier League champions United and FA Cup winners Portsmouth play out 90 minutes without either side scoring, meaning the 2008 FA Community Shield must be settled on penalties at Wembley.

- Lassana Diarra (Portsmouth) misses – 0-0
- Carlos Tevez (Manchester United) scores – 0-1
- Jermain Defoe (Portsmouth) scores – 1-1
- Ryan Giggs (Manchester United) scores – 1-2
- Arnold Mvuemba (Portsmouth) misses – 1-2
- Michael Carrick (Manchester United) scores – 1-3
- Glen Johnson (Portsmouth) misses – 1-3

Manchester United win 3-1 on penalties

1 March 2009

United and Tottenham Hotspur cannot be separated in the League Cup Final at Wembley, drawing 0-0 after 90 minutes, and with no goals during extra time, the game had to be settled by a penalty shoot-out – only the second time the League Cup had been decided in this fashion.

- Ryan Giggs (Manchester United) scores – 1-0
- Jamie O'Hara (Tottenham Hotspur) misses – 1-0
- Carlos Tevez (Manchester United) scores – 2-0
- Vedran Corluka (Tottenham Hotspur) scores – 2-1
- Cristiano Ronaldo (Manchester United) scores – 3-1
- David Bentley (Tottenham Hotspur) misses – 3-1
- Anderson (Manchester United) scores – 4-1

Manchester United win 4-1 on penalties

25 September 2018

Having scored a last-gasp added-time leveller to make it 2-2 against Championship side Derby County, United have the opportunity to progress instead via a penalty shoot-out against the Rams.

- Mason Mount (Derby County) scores – 1-0
- Romelu Lukaku (Manchester United) scores – 1-1
- Florian Jozefzoon (Derby County) scores – 2-1
- Ashley Young (Manchester United) scores – 2-2
- Harry Wilson (Derby County) scores – 3-2
- Marouane Fellaini (Manchester United) scores – 3-3
- Jack Marriott (Derby County) scores – 4-3
- Fred (Manchester United) scores – 4-4
- Bradley Johnson (Derby County) scores – 5-4
- Anthony Martial (Manchester United) scores – 5-5
- Craig Bryson (Derby County) scores – 6-5
- Diogo Dalot (Manchester United) scores – 6-6
- Craig Forsyth (Derby County) scores – 7-6
- Nemanja Matic (Manchester United) scores 7-7
- Richard Keogh (Derby County) scores – 8-7
- Phil Jones (Manchester United) misses – 8-7

Derby County win 8-7 on penalties

25 September 2019

After being held by League One side Rochdale in normal time, United are forced into a penalty shoot-out at Old Trafford for the right to move into the League Cup fourth round.

- Juan Mata (Manchester United) scores – 1-0
- Calvin Andrew (Rochdale) scores – 1-1
- Andreas Pereira (Manchester United) scores – 2-1
- Jimmy Keohane (Rochdale) misses – 2-1
- Fred (Manchester United) scores – 3-1
- Aaron Morley (Rochdale) scores – 3-2
- Mason Greenwood (Manchester United) scores – 4-2
- Aaron Wilbraham (Rochdale) scores – 4-3
- Daniel James (Manchester United) scores 5-3

Manchester United win 5-3 on penalties

Also available at all good book stores

9781909626409

9781909178755

9781908051783

9781908051684

9781908051813

9781785310041

9781785314698

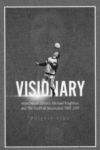

9781785315770

9781785313974